VENISON
Every Day

THE NO-FUSS GUIDE TO COOKING GAME AT HOME

VENISON
Every Day

Allie Doran

FOUNDER OF
MISS ALLIE'S KITCHEN

PAGE STREET
PUBLISHING CO.

PAGE STREET
PUBLISHING CO.

First published in 2020 by

Page Street Publishing Co.

27 Congress Street, Suite 105

Salem, MA 01970

www.pagestreetpublishing.com

Distributed by Macmillan, sales in Canada by The Canadian Manda Group.

24   23   22   21   20   1   2   3   4   5

ISBN-13: 978-1-64567-124-4

ISBN-10: 1-64567-124-0

Library of Congress Control Number: 2019957253

Cover and book design by Laura Benton for Page Street Publishing Co.

Photography by Allie Doran

Printed and bound in China

For Jared.

None of this would be possible without you.
Thank you for being my rock, biggest supporter
and sounding board. I love you endlessly.

Contents

Introduction & How to Use This Book

Welcome, new friend! I'm Allie, an extroverted food writer and photographer, and—you guessed it—I'm pretty obsessed with food. I also happen to be an accidental hunter's wife.

What does it mean to be an accidental hunter's wife, you ask? If you told me ten years ago that I would have two freezers full of wild game in my home, I would have looked at you a little funny. I grew up in a household where we ate beef, pork and A LOT of chicken.

When I met my husband, Jared, I instantly fell for him. He has been an avid hunter since about age eight, and I have since grown quite fond of the outdoor lifestyle we now live.

After I met Jared, I quickly found myself with a lot of deer meat on my hands. Being a food writer, the seemingly natural thing for me to do was to cook with it. And in the beginning, it wasn't so easy.

When I started cooking with venison, I found that most of the recipes I came across were either wildly outdated and/or fried and unhealthy. The others were extremely technical and developed by chefs. I'm a highly experienced recipe developer, and even I thought they had too many steps. Nothing I found would be something that I could whip up in 30 minutes on a weeknight or confidently serve to guests.

My husband is the primary hunter in our household, and like many hunters and outdoor enthusiasts, we believe respecting our harvest to be most important. To us, this means using as much of the animal we kill as possible. But in the early years, I found that we were wasting pounds and pounds of beautiful venison every year because we didn't know how to use it in our everyday meals. This gnawed at the back of my brain.

So, I took to the kitchen. Little by little, I learned about cooking with our deer meat. I gathered tips and tricks through research, trial and lots of error.

Years later, I decided to write a cookbook all about using more of and respecting a deer after its life has been taken. This book was written not only to use up the meat I have in the freezer, but also to show you how to work with all the different cuts of meat from the animal. It reflects how we eat in our home; sometimes gluten and dairy free, sometimes not, but our meals always have lean protein and veggies involved. There is so much more to venison than chili and sausage!

This book is everything I wish I had known when I met my husband and started cooking with venison. There isn't much out there directed at home cooks who end up working with deer meat once it comes into the house after a hunt. Whether you're an avid hunter looking to get more out of your freezer stash or a family member of a hunter (like me) who happens to be the primary cook in the household, this is exactly what you need to get ideas and answers to all of those burning questions I know you have!

All of the recipes in this book have been created by a home cook and professional recipe developer who happens to be an accidental hunter's wife—me! They represent my cooking style—fresh, bold flavors, healthier twists and plenty of updated comfort food. I've developed them all to be foolproof and to encourage you to start using venison every day. The final chapter (page 135) contains side dishes, or recipes without venison, like biscuits, pastry dough and vegetables, because I want you to be able to have the makings of a complete meal right from this cookbook.

Imagine what it would be like to have your family gobble up meal after meal with deer meat and serve beautiful cuts of venison to guests at the holidays—and have them sing your praises. Not only will you be more responsible with your venison, but your wallet will also thank you, because you'll be spending less money on meat at the store. Doesn't that sound like a dream?

I wrote this book for those of you who are learning to cook with your harvest or are sick of the same old recipes you always make. I'll make a promise to you—this book and these recipes will change your life. This isn't just your standard cookbook. *Venison Every Day* was written to give you knowledge and actionable steps so you can confidently cook with your harvest every day.

Cut Cheat Sheet

1. NECK–best for roasts and ground meat. It has a lot of connective tissue and fat throughout the meat, so it's great for braising because all of that gets melted when you cook it low and slow. I also like using it for pulled meat like barbacoa or for sandwiches. For this cut, try my Barbacoa Meat on page 47.

2. SHOULDER–best for roasts. Do your best to keep these whole and resist processing them into ground meat. Deer shoulders are perfect for roasting, braising or even making cured meats like pastrami. Brisket also comes from the lower chest or the bottom of the shoulder of an animal. For this cut, try my Perfect Roast with Garlic & Herbs on page 19.

3. LOIN–this is also known as the backstrap and it runs along the backbone of the deer. A lot of people confuse the tenderloin and the backstrap, but the loin/backstrap is a bit larger and can be a little less tender. It's still a lovely cut of meat that is great for steaks. Many people cut these into chops, and while this is fine, they're often overcooked in preparation. It's best to leave them whole when you can. For this cut, try my Soy-Glazed Medallions on page 24.

4. RUMP–for steaks or roasts. If you're a big fan of roasts, this is another part of the animal that can be left in one or several large pieces. For this cut, try my Chimichurri-Marinated Steak with Fresh Salsa on page 51.

5. SIRLOIN–best for steaks and jerky. Leg steaks can be a bit sinewy, so be sure to marinate and use plenty of salt, fat and acid to break that down. For this cut, use my All-Purpose Marinade on page 123.

6. TENDERLOIN–keep this whole if you can and use it as a roasted tenderloin or chop. This is arguably the most sought-after cut of the entire deer. It's quite literally the filet mignon of venison. For this cut, try my Roasted Whole Tenderloin with Peppercorns on page 31.

7. FORELEG–for jerky or potentially steak, but your best bet may be ground. If you have a huge deer, you may be able to get some awesome steaks, but this cut may be best turned into ground meat with a leaner or smaller deer. For this cut, try my Kebabs with Tahini-Yogurt Sauce on page 43.

8. RIBS–do not ever let your deer ribs be made into ground meat. They are my favorite cut of venison, not even kidding. Get them broken into four to eight ribs per piece and braise them. For this cut, try my Red Wine–Braised Short Ribs with Herb Gremolata on page 35.

9. F L A N K – best for jerky or steaks. These are super flavorful, but they can be very dry and tough. If you're going to cook with them, cube them up and put them in tacos, kebabs, etc. Be sure to use one of my marinades, too! For this cut, try my Easiest Black Pepper Jerky on page 66.

10. T R I M – potentially roasts, jerky or ground, depending on the size of the animal and your goals. Try ground meat with my Classic Italian Meatballs on page 44.

11. S H A N K – this needs slow and low roasting. Try my method for making Red Wine–Braised Short Ribs with Herb Gremolata on page 35 with this cut for tender, fall-off-the-bone deliciousness.

12. S H I N – same as for shank. For more ground meat ideas, try the Asian Chop Salad on page 91.

Field-to-Freezer Prep

When Jared and I first met, he would come home from the butcher with deer meat wrapped in butcher paper and a load of ground meat in a huge plastic bag. The cuts wrapped in the paper would go directly into the freezer, and we would eyeball the ground meat out into 2-pound (910-g) portions and seal them in zip-top baggies.

Doesn't sound very efficient, does it? Let me tell you how we do things differently now.

HOW TO PROPERLY FIELD DRESS A DEER

The first step after a successful hunt is properly field dressing your deer so you can bring it home or to a butcher to process. This is extremely important because mishandling a deer can make it unsafe to eat or taint the flavor.

Once you harvest your animal, you first want to evaluate your shot placement. Obviously, your goal is to hit a vital organ, which would result in a quick and ethical kill. However, a low shot made in the abdomen could also rupture the intestines and taint the meat, making your job in the field a bit more challenging. If you find yourself with an animal that has ruptured intestines, you'll want to take extra precautions to clean any waste from the animal before you start to break it down.

Assuming you have a clean kill, after assessing the shot, flip the deer on its back so the belly is facing up. It's helpful to have a friend or two to help with this. You'll also need to make sure you have a sharp knife. Then, make an incision starting down at the lower pelvic area and bring your knife up to the chest cavity. Take care not to cut into the intestines during this process.

Next, flip the deer back on its side so that the entrails are expelled from the body. You can cut through any remaining tissue or membranes to help with this. The goal is to remove all of the internal organs: liver, heart, intestines, lungs, bladder, kidney, diaphragm and stomach. It's up to you if you'd like to keep the heart, liver and kidneys. Then, remove the deer from the harvest site and take it for processing.

ON PROCESSING YOUR DEER—DIY OR BUTCHER

Processing your deer is when you break down the animal into cuts of meat. You can do this yourself or have a trusted butcher do it for you. If you decide to do this yourself, it's important to have a large, sterile workspace to prepare the meat.

Once you decide how you're going to process the animal, take another look at the cut sheet (see page 10) so you can decide exactly what you want out of the animal. The first thing I do before my husband goes hunting is draft a shared note on my phone of my cut list requests. That way, when he harvests a deer, he has a quick reference guide of exactly what I want when he takes the animal from the field to the butcher. This has helped us tremendously because I'm the primary cook in the household, and he doesn't know exactly which cuts I use for what dishes. There's no guessing game: we go in with a plan.

STORING VENISON

Once you have your meat processed and at home, clear some counter space and get out a kitchen scale, a vacuum sealer and a permanent marker. I like to weigh my roasts, steaks and larger cuts so I know their weight when cooking them. Weight affects cooking time and serving yields. I also like to weigh out any ground meat into 1-pound (455-g) portions for ease when cooking.

It's best to store meat in vacuum-sealed and labeled bags. When you're ready to cook, either remove the meat from the freezer a day or two before or thaw the meat in a bowl of cool water.

Properly harvesting, field dressing, processing and storing venison can make all the difference when cooking with deer meat. It ensures that the flavors are clean and that the meat lasts. It's always a good idea to enlist the help of someone more experienced when hunting or working with a harvested animal, so make sure you get some help if you need it.

Troubleshooting, Tips & Tricks

I often say that if deer could talk, they would say this when people complain about the dry, gamey meat they prepare: "It's not me, it's you." The first hard-and-fast rule is that if you're complaining about an offensive taste from your meat, it's probably because it was mishandled either in the field or in the kitchen.

Properly killing, gutting, quartering and processing an animal is crucial, as I explained earlier. A clean, swift kill cuts down on the amount of stress hormones an animal releases. A lot of hormones in a deer's blood will affect the taste. This is also why a lot of buck harvested by trophy hunters, or hunters who harvest mature, large buck during rutting (mating) season (like my husband), have meat that can taste a bit stronger than that from a young deer. There are more hormones present in the bloodstream during the time of harvest.

However, harvesting a mature buck is conducive to population control in many areas, so this is something that can't often be avoided. We'll talk about strategies to cut down on the stronger flavor of mature meat later in this chapter.

In any case, the number one rule for harvesting the best-tasting meat is this: Make sure whoever processes your deer in the field knows what they're doing. When field dressing a deer, it is very important to have someone who is knowledgeable present. Improperly doing this step in your harvest can taint the meat, significantly altering the flavor to something that no amount of good cooking can fix. Properly harvested and field-dressed venison shouldn't be smelly or outrightly offensive to the taste buds when cooked to medium-rare.

TIP #1: DON'T OVERCOOK THE MEAT

This brings me to my first tip when it comes to cooking with venison: Do not overcook the meat. When cooking venison steaks, tenderloin, backstraps, chops and even some leg roasts, you want a rare to medium-rare internal temperature. This is between 120 and 130°F (49 and 54°C). Getting a really good instant-read meat thermometer is crucial here.

When people talk about that iron-like "gamey" flavor, it's most likely because the meat is overcooked. I know many people like their meat to at least medium, but I strongly recommend getting used to eating your venison (and some other wild game meat) at medium-rare.

On another note, when your food comes to 120 to 125°F (49 to 52°C), remove it from the heat and cover it with foil to rest for about 10 minutes before serving. Resting is so, so important when cooking any meat because it draws the juices back in.

TIP #2: SEASON DISHES PROPERLY

Make sure your food has enough salt! Almost every single one of the dishes in this book has exact seasoning ratios. I'm not really one to measure out salt and pepper when cooking for my family, but I made sure to nail down exactly how much you need for each recipe so you know you're cooking a meal that has balanced flavors. By making sure your dish has enough salt and pepper, you enhance the naturally delicious flavors of the meat.

TIP #3: ADD FAT

Most people add bacon or pork fat to ground meat during processing, which is always a great idea in my opinion. But when working with larger cuts of meat or steaks, a marinade with plenty of fat (I usually opt for olive oil) can really help. Choose a high-quality fat to add to marinades or while cooking dishes.

TIPS #4: ADD ACID

This is my favorite way to combat that rich flavor that many mature buck carry with them. I add acid to almost everything I cook with venison. This is also a great way to change up a family-favorite recipe you usually make with beef, such as chili or meatballs. Just add 1 to 2 tablespoons (15 to 30 ml) of citrus juice or balsamic, apple cider, white or red wine vinegar to whatever you're making.

All of the sauces and marinades in this book have a healthy amount of acid in them, and you'll love what they do to the flavor of the meat. Acid also helps break down connective tissue, giving you more tender meat. If I had to pick the most valuable tip, this would be it.

TIP #5: REMOVE THE SINEW

Talking about tissue brings me to my last tip. Deer are very lean, spindly and active animals and have a lot of sinew or connective tissue. This is that silvery or white stretchy stuff you often see weaving its way through meat. Cooking pieces of meat with a lot of sinew causes the meat to curl up and get rubbery.

If you have a piece of meat with a lot of sinew, such as a leg steak, it's best to chop it up into cubes and remove the connective tissue. Or roast it low and slow, as you would do with a neck roast, which will help melt the sinew. But I find that it's usually easy to just cut it out and discard or save the scraps for stock, if possible.

COOKING DELICIOUS DEER MEAT IS JUST GOOD COOKING

If you've heard a lot of these tips before from chefs, on TV or in cookbooks, it's because they're principals of good cooking. Acid, fat, salt, heat—sound familiar?

Take care when cooking with your harvest, and you'll be well on your way to having delicious meals with venison every day. You can do this!

Classic Comfort Food Dinners

I love making comfort food. There's nothing like serving someone a cozy hug on a plate, and this first chapter is exactly that.

These recipes give you that warm and fuzzy feeling all over, and many of them are perfect for the holidays. I like to put updated and healthier spins on a lot of the dishes I make, and you'll find that it only makes the recipe more interesting and delicious.

Welcome to my favorite chapter of this book!

Perfect Roast with Garlic & Herbs

SERVES 6 TO 8

GLUTEN FREE | DAIRY FREE

There are few things better, easier and more impressive than a good roast. And I'm begging you—if you're not leaving your rump, neck and/or shoulder roasts whole, start doing so! You won't be sorry. This recipe is very similar to traditional beef roast. I use a little lemon zest and balsamic vinegar to add brightness and help tenderize the meat. The smells that fill your house when you make this are absolutely heavenly. You won't believe how tender venison can actually be.

3 lb (1.4 kg) roast (if your roast is smaller or larger, you may need to adjust the cooking time)

1 tsp salt

1 tsp pepper

2 tbsp (30 ml) olive oil

4 cloves garlic, minced

½ tsp lemon zest

2 tsp (2 g) fresh thyme leaves

2 tsp (2 g) chopped fresh rosemary

1 cup (240 ml) beef or venison stock, homemade (page 124) or store-bought

½ cup (120 ml) dry red wine or more stock

2 tbsp (30 ml) balsamic vinegar

3 tbsp (45 g) tomato paste

Preheat the oven to 350°F (180°C).

Heat a Dutch oven or large pan over medium-high heat. I prefer to use a Dutch oven because I can cook the roast in it the entire time, but if you don't have one, use a large pan to sear the meat and then roast it in a covered roasting dish.

Rub the roast all over with the salt and pepper and add the oil to the pan. Sear the venison on each side to create a nice, brown crust all over the meat. This will take 4 to 7 minutes per side.

Once the venison is seared, remove it from the heat. If you're not using a Dutch oven, transfer the roast to a roasting pan.

In a medium bowl, mix together the garlic, lemon zest, thyme, rosemary, stock, red wine, vinegar and tomato paste and pour it all over the roast, making sure every bit of it has been touched by the liquid.

Cover the roast either with a lid or foil and bake for about 2½ to 3 hours, or until the roast is very tender. If you want, reserve the pan juices for serving.

Classic Shepherd's Pie

Shepherd's pie is a fan favorite in our house. I mean, beer, potatoes and meat all in one dish—what more do you want?! Shepherd's pie is much easier to make than it gets credit for. It's really just a hearty ground meat filling topped with perfectly whipped potatoes. It hangs out in the oven until the top gets nice and crusty. Sláinte!

5 tbsp (75 g) butter, divided

1 large yellow onion, diced

1½ cups (192 g) diced carrot

1½ cups (150 g) diced celery

1 lb (455 g) ground venison

3 cloves garlic, minced

2 tsp (12 g) salt, divided

1½ tsp (2 g) pepper, divided

1 tsp dried thyme

½ tsp ground sage

1 cup (240 ml) dark beer, like Guinness or a stout

2 tsp (10 ml) apple cider vinegar

1 (6-oz [168-g]) can tomato paste

1 cup (134 g) frozen peas

3 lbs (1.4 kg) gold potatoes (7 or 8 medium potatoes), peeled if desired

1 cup (240 ml) milk, warmed

Preheat the oven to 400°F (200°C). Grease a 9 x 13–inch (23 x 33–cm) casserole dish.

Put a large pot of water on to boil the potatoes in.

Heat 1 tablespoon (15 g) of the butter in a large skillet over medium heat. Add the onion, carrot and celery and sauté until they start to soften, about 8 minutes.

Add the ground venison and cook, stirring occasionally, until the venison is browned, about 10 minutes. Add the garlic, ½ teaspoon of the salt, 1 teaspoon of the pepper, thyme and sage. Sauté, stirring, for 2 minutes to let the spices release their flavor.

Add the beer and vinegar and allow the alcohol to cook off, about 5 minutes. Stir in the tomato paste. Bring the mixture to a boil, lower the heat and simmer for 10 to 15 minutes while you prepare the potatoes. When you're ready to assemble the dish, remove the pan from the heat and stir in the frozen peas.

When your water is boiling, cube the potatoes and carefully add them to the pot. Boil them for about 15 minutes, until they're nice and soft. Drain and add the potatoes to a large bowl or the bowl of a stand mixer. Whip the potatoes with a handheld mixer (or by hand) or in the stand mixer, and add the remaining 4 tablespoons (60 g) of butter, 1½ teaspoons (9 g) of salt and ½ teaspoon of pepper. Gradually add the milk until you get the texture you want. I like my potatoes to be a little thinner than mashed potatoes for this dish. It helps the topping get nice and crispy.

Spoon the meat filling into the prepared casserole dish, and then top it with the whipped potatoes. Smooth the potatoes out into an even layer.

Bake the shepherd's pie for 20 to 25 minutes, until the top is golden brown and the filling is bubbly.

Chipotle Jack Burgers with Easy Chipotle Mayo

SERVES 4

30 MINUTES OR LESS

Venison and chipotle are a match made in heaven, and my love knows no bounds when it comes to these burgers.

I use the juice from a can of chipotle peppers to flavor the ground meat, and the chipotle peppers get added to the mayo. The flavor is incredible, and the mayo is super simple to make in a blender or food processor. Burger night just got ridiculous.

½ cup (120 ml) mayonnaise

½ tsp lemon juice

1 (7-oz [196-g]) can chipotle peppers, divided

1 clove garlic

1 lb (455 g) ground venison

½ tsp salt

½ tsp black pepper

1 cup (113 g) shredded or 4 slices pepper Jack cheese

4 buns (we love brioche)

About 2 cups (60 g) shredded lettuce

1 tomato, sliced

Before you make the burgers, preheat a skillet over medium-high heat or preheat a grill to medium-high heat. You want a nice, hot surface to cook your burgers on.

While the skillet preheats, add the mayonnaise, lemon juice, 2 of the chipotle peppers and the garlic to a blender or small food processor. Blend until combined and smooth. Set the chipotle mayo aside or place it in the fridge until you're ready to assemble the burgers.

To form the burgers, add the venison to a bowl. Drain the chipotle juice from the can into the bowl to flavor the meat. Save the remaining peppers for another recipe. Add the salt and pepper to the bowl and mix well so the seasonings and chipotle juice are evenly distributed in the meat.

Form four evenly sized patties and place them on the skillet or grill. Cook the burgers for about 5 minutes per side, adding the cheese when you flip to the second side, until the burgers are medium, about 145°F (63°C) internally on a meat thermometer.

Remove the patties from the heat and begin to build your burgers! Spread even amounts of the chipotle mayo on the buns. Add the patties and top with the lettuce and tomato and any other desired toppings.

Soy-Glazed Medallions

When it comes to venison tenderloin, simple is best. Marinating it in a simple mixture of seasoning, oil and soy sauce gives it the perfect touch of flavor without overpowering the meat.

You're going to cook your meat to medium-rare—I insist that you try it. Overcooking venison is kind of a crime in my book. That's when you get that dry gaminess that no one likes. So, trust me on this.

This pairs perfectly with my Best Ever Stovetop Broccoli (page 146).

1 lb (455 g) venison tenderloin medallions (or slice a tenderloin to create 1" [2.5-cm]-thick slices)

2 tbsp (30 ml) soy sauce (or coconut aminos for soy/gluten free)

1 tbsp (15 ml) olive oil

¾ tsp pepper

Add the venison, soy sauce and oil to a zip-top bag or bowl. Make sure all of the venison is covered with the marinade. Marinate the meat in the fridge for at least 30 minutes or up to 1 day.

When you're ready to cook, remove the venison from the fridge and let it come to room temperature to ensure even cooking.

Heat a large skillet over medium-high heat. Add the venison to the heated pan and cook for 2 to 3 minutes per side until it's medium-rare, 125 to 130°F (52 to 54°C) on a meat thermometer.

Immediately remove the medallions from the pan and let them rest on a plate, brushing them with the pan juices. Sprinkle with the pepper and serve.

NOTE: The soy sauce should make the meat salty enough, but make sure there's salt on the table to add if not.

Swedish Meatballs

SERVES 4

Many people associate Swedish meatballs with the Swedish company IKEA, but like many things (such as French fries), the name doesn't accurately depict their origin. To be honest, all I know is that these little babies are GOOD, and I would endure countless hours of putting together IKEA furniture to have some of them. If you've ever had to build anything from there, then you know what a bold statement that is. Ground venison is a welcome flavor to the rich broth and perfectly flavored meatballs! Serve over egg noodles or spaghetti squash.

FOR THE MEATBALLS

1 lb (455 g) ground venison

½ lb (224 g) ground pork

½ onion, minced

Juice of ½ lemon

1 tsp Dijon mustard

2 tsp (8 g) coconut sugar

1 tsp salt

1 tsp garlic powder

½ tsp pepper

Pinch of nutmeg

1 egg, beaten

¼ cup (25 g) almond meal or bread crumbs

FOR THE GRAVY

3 tbsp (45 g) butter

½ onion, minced

¼ cup (31 g) all-purpose flour

¾ tsp salt

½ tsp pepper

3 cups (720 ml) beef broth

3 or 4 dashes of Worcestershire sauce

2 tbsp (30 ml) sour cream

Egg noodles or spaghetti squash, to serve

To make the meatballs, preheat the oven to 400°F (200°C) and line a baking sheet with foil or a Silpat.

Add all of the ingredients for the meatballs to a large bowl and mix them together until everything is well incorporated. I like to do this with my hands and a fork.

Using a large cookie scoop, scoop the meatball mixture and roll them between your hands to make them evenly shaped. Arrange the meatballs on the prepared baking sheet so that they don't touch each other. Bake the meatballs for 18 minutes, then remove them from the oven and set aside.

To make the gravy, while the meatballs bake, add the butter to a large saucepan and let it melt over medium heat. Add the onion and sauté until it starts to brown, 5 to 6 minutes. Add the flour, salt and pepper and cook, stirring, for 3 minutes to cook out the raw flour taste. Add the beef broth and whisk the gravy constantly until no clumps of flour remain. Add the Worcestershire sauce and keep whisking the gravy, scraping the edges of the pan frequently.

Once the gravy starts to bubble and thicken to the desired consistency, add the sour cream and stir it in completely. Remove the saucepan from the heat and add the meatballs. Spoon the gravy over the meatballs so they're all covered. Serve over egg noodles or spaghetti squash

Slow Cooker Brisket Sandwiches

SERVES 4
DAIRY-FREE OPTION

I love to get brisket cut from venison and make my own brisket sandwiches at home. The easiest way to do this is in the slow cooker. Brisket generally comes from the lower chest or the bottom of the shoulder of an animal. It's typically pretty lean meat, with a cap of fat on top if you're working with fattier meat like beef, but with venison, it's very lean and it's an awesome source of protein. It works perfectly when it's seared and then slow cooked. The meat is wonderful when reheated and can be prepared several days before you need it, and this makes for great leftovers.

1 tsp olive oil

2 lb (910 g) brisket (a roast would also work)

1 small yellow onion, thinly sliced

3 cloves garlic, minced

½ cup (120 ml) beer (I used a dark milk stout)

2 tsp (8 g) coconut sugar

1 tbsp (15 g) tomato paste

1 tbsp (15 ml) balsamic vinegar

2 tsp (10 ml) Dijon mustard

1 tsp soy sauce (or coconut aminos for soy free)

½ tsp salt

¼ tsp black pepper

4 crusty white sub rolls

OPTIONAL TOPPINGS

Provolone cheese (omit if eating dairy free)

Roasted red peppers

Cooked broccoli rabe (see Note)

Start by searing the brisket to add some flavor. Add the oil to a large skillet (use cast iron if you have it) over medium-high heat. When the pan is hot, add the brisket and sear each side for 3 to 5 minutes. There should be a nice brown crust on the meat. You may have to do this in batches depending on the size of your meat and pan.

Place the brisket into a slow cooker and set it to high. Add the onion, garlic, beer, coconut sugar, tomato paste, balsamic vinegar, mustard, soy sauce, salt and pepper. After about 2 hours, turn the slow cooker to low and allow the brisket to cook and get tender for 4 to 5 hours. Once the meat is tender, shred the brisket with forks.

When you're ready to serve, get out the rolls and the toppings of your choice!

NOTE: To cook the broccoli rabe, fill a large saucepan halfway with water and bring to a boil. Meanwhile, prepare an ice water bath. Add the broccoli rabe to the boiling water and cook for 30 seconds, then immediately transfer it to the ice water bath. Pour the water out of the saucepan. Place the saucepan back over medium heat and add 1 tablespoon (15 ml) of oil to the pan. Once the oil is hot, add the broccoli rabe and cook for 4 to 5 minutes, until tender. Season with salt and pepper to taste.

Roasted Whole Tenderloin with Peppercorns

SERVES 6 TO 8
GLUTEN FREE | DAIRY FREE

This peppercorn tenderloin is really something. I like to reserve this for a special night or the holidays because it's easy to whip up for guests, but it's very impressive. The result is a very tender and flavorful piece of venison. It's best served with my Blueberry Balsamic Reduction (page 131) and Herb Roasted Potatoes (page 145).

2 to 3 lb (910 g to 1.4 kg) whole venison tenderloin (or backstrap will work)

2 tbsp (6 g) coarsely cracked fresh peppercorns

2 tsp (12 g) salt

5 cloves garlic, minced

2 tsp (4 g) lemon zest

½ tsp chopped fresh thyme

About 30 minutes before you're ready to cook, remove the venison from the fridge and let it come to room temperature to ensure even cooking.

Preheat the oven to 450°F (230°C) and set out a large roasting pan.

In a small bowl, mix together the peppercorns, salt, garlic, lemon zest and thyme. Press this spice mixture onto the tenderloin, covering the entire piece of meat.

Place the tenderloin in the roasting pan and cook it in the oven for 15 minutes. After the 15 minutes is up, remove the pan from the oven and take the temperature of the meat. You want it to be 120 to 130°F (49 to 54°C) for medium-rare. Place the pan back in the oven for 5-minute increments until a medium-rare temperature is reached, 5 to 10 more minutes.

Remove the tenderloin from the oven and let it rest for at least 10 to 15 minutes before slicing and serving.

Lightened-Up Stroganoff

SERVES 4 TO 6

Nothing is more comforting than a big plate of stroganoff. What could be better than a creamy, earthy sauce over egg noodles? Traditional stroganoff is very heavy, with lots of butter and sour cream. I love those ingredients, but we generally try to eat a bit lighter most days.

I make a few swaps (coconut milk and Greek yogurt, mainly), but the result is a silky smooth dish with lots of flavor. If you want to lighten things up further and add some veggies to the mix, serve this over butternut squash noodles.

1 tbsp (15 g) butter

1 tbsp (15 ml) olive oil

1 yellow onion, diced

1 lb (455 g) ground venison

8 oz (228 g) baby bella mushrooms, stemmed and sliced

2 cloves garlic, minced

¾ tsp salt

½ tsp pepper

¼ tsp paprika

Pinch of dried thyme

2 tbsp (16 g) arrowroot powder, cornstarch or tapioca starch

¼ cup (60 ml) dry white wine or beef broth (use wine if you can—this is key to the flavor)

1 tbsp (15 ml) apple cider vinegar

¾ cup (180 ml) full-fat coconut milk

1 cup (240 ml) beef broth

3 to 5 dashes of Worcestershire sauce

½ cup (120 ml) plain Greek yogurt (we like full fat, but any will do)

Egg noodles, gluten-free noodles or butternut squash noodles, for serving

Heat the butter and olive oil in a large pot over medium heat until the butter is melted. Add the onion and cook for 3 to 5 minutes, or until slightly brown and translucent. Add the ground venison and cook, stirring occasionally, until the venison is browned, about 8 minutes.

Add the mushrooms, garlic, salt, pepper, paprika and thyme and cook for 2 minutes to release the flavors. Add the arrowroot powder and cook, stirring, for 2 additional minutes to combine everything well.

Add the wine and apple cider vinegar and cook for 2 minutes, scraping up all the bits at the bottom of the pan. That's where the flavor is! Add the coconut milk, beef broth and Worcestershire sauce. Let the mixture come to a boil, cover, lower the heat and simmer for 10 minutes.

Add the yogurt, stir well to combine and cook the stroganoff for just 2 more minutes. Remove the pot from the heat. Serve with your choice of noodles.

Red Wine–Braised Short Ribs with Herb Gremolata

SERVES 4 TO 6

GLUTEN FREE | DAIRY FREE

Short ribs are my favorite thing to make on Christmas Day. I love them because you can make them a day or two beforehand and then just slide them in the fridge, in the vessel you cook them in, until you're ready to serve. Then they simply get heated up, and voilà—a really beautiful and cozy dish! It should be noted that deer short ribs are best from larger deer. I highly recommend leaving at least half of your ribs whole so you can try out short ribs. You'll be blown away with how tender they are! I like to serve this with polenta and plenty of the pan juices.

2 lbs (910 g) venison ribs

4 cloves garlic, minced

2 tsp (2 g) chopped fresh rosemary, plus 2 whole sprigs, divided

2 tsp (2 g) chopped fresh thyme

Zest from 1 lemon

2½ tsp (15 g) salt, divided

2 tsp (4 g) pepper

1 tbsp (15 ml) olive oil

2 cups (480 ml) dry red wine, such as Cabernet, or beef broth

2 cups (480 ml) beef or venison broth

1 tbsp (15 ml) apple cider vinegar

2 tbsp (30 g) tomato paste

The night before you want to make the short ribs, place them on a cutting board and cut the ribs into smaller pieces, with about 4 ribs per piece. This makes searing them much easier.

In a bowl, mix together the garlic, chopped rosemary, thyme, lemon zest, 1 teaspoon of the salt and pepper to make the herb gremolata. Rub about three-fourths of the gremolata all over the short ribs and place them in an airtight container in the fridge. Let the short ribs sit overnight to absorb the flavors of the gremolata. Store the remaining gremolata in a separate container in the fridge.

The next day, preheat the oven to 325°F (170°C). Set out a Dutch oven or 9 x 13–inch (23 x 33–cm) baking dish.

Remove the short ribs from the fridge and brush off some of the gremolata.

Heat the olive oil in a Dutch oven or large skillet over medium-high heat. Add the short ribs and sear on both sides so that there's a nice, golden brown crust. Set the short ribs aside and wipe out the pan.

Turn the heat down to medium-low and add the wine, broth, vinegar, tomato paste and remaining 1½ teaspoons (9 g) of salt to the pan. Whisk until the tomato paste has dissolved into the liquid. Turn off the heat.

If you're using a Dutch oven, add the short ribs back and spoon the liquid all over them. If you're using a baking dish, add the short ribs to the dish and pour over the red wine sauce. Place the remaining rosemary sprigs over the short ribs and cover the Dutch oven with the lid or the dish with foil. Bake for about 2 hours. The meat should be falling off the bone. Discard the rosemary sprigs.

Before serving, sprinkle the remaining gremolata all over the short ribs.

Globally Inspired Mains

I get a lot of inspiration from different cultures or places around the world. With wild game, I find that it can stand up to strong and unique flavors, so I often find myself making globally inspired meals with venison.

You'll see in this chapter that there are some staple recipes, like meatballs, Italian sausage and chorizo, that get used in a variety of recipes in this book. These are pillars in my kitchen, and I like to have versatile recipes I can make a lot of dishes with! This chapter will be an eye-opener for you if you're looking to add some new deer meat recipes to your rotation.

Venison Chorizo

If you asked me to pick one type of cuisine to eat for the rest of my life, I'd have to go with Mexican. Chorizo is a coveted meat in our house, as is anything with a bit of spice and heat.

I thought making chorizo out of venison would be perfect for those who don't absolutely LOVE the flavor of deer meat because chorizo has plenty of acid and seasoning plus a bit of pork fat to tone down the richer flavor. You can make this and cook it right away, or freeze it cooked or raw and use as needed. You'll find several recipes in this book that call for it.

1 lb (455 g) ground venison

½ lb (226 g) ground pork

⅓ cup (80 ml) apple cider vinegar

Juice of 1 lime

3 tbsp (18 g) chili powder

2 tbsp (12 g) paprika

1 tsp salt

1 tsp ground cinnamon

1 tsp dried thyme

1 tsp dried oregano

½ tsp pepper

Pinch of ground cloves

Add all of the ingredients to a large bowl. Using your hands or a spoon (I always use my hands), mix everything together well so that the venison, pork, spices and seasonings are all incorporated. You want the spices to be well distributed.

When you're ready to cook the ground chorizo, simply add the mixture to a saucepan with 1 tablespoon (15 ml) of oil and cook over medium heat until browned, about 10 minutes.

Once cooled, store it in the fridge for up to 2 days or in the freezer for up to 3 months in an airtight container or freezer bag. Alternatively, you can freeze the uncooked chorizo if you're working with meat that you just harvested (see Note).

NOTE: I wouldn't recommend thawing frozen venison, mixing this up and then freezing it raw again. If you're using older venison, go ahead and brown it and use it within a few days or freeze it precooked.

Italian Sausage

Italian sausage is another staple I always find myself picking up when I'm at the store. It's really versatile and I prefer it to be out of the casing.

With an abundance of ground venison on hand, I went to the drawing board. No need to buy the store-bought stuff when I can make my own with free-range, grass-fed protein. You can make this and cook it right away, or freeze it raw and use it as needed. As I said, I prefer Italian sausage out of the casing, so there's no need to use any fancy machines—just mix it all together and use it whenever you need Italian sausage or in any of the recipes that call for it in this book!

1 lb (455 g) ground venison

½ lb (226 g) ground pork

1 tbsp (4 g) chopped fresh parsley

2 tsp (8 g) coconut or brown sugar

¾ tsp salt

¾ tsp black pepper

1 tsp garlic powder

1 tsp onion powder

1 tsp paprika

½ tsp crushed red pepper flakes

¼ tsp dried thyme

¼ tsp dried oregano

Add all of the ingredients to a large bowl. Using your hands or a spoon (I recommend using your hands), mix everything together well so that the venison, pork, spices and seasonings are all incorporated. You want the spices to be well distributed.

When you're ready to cook the sausage, simply add the mixture to a saucepan with 1 tablespoon (15 ml) of oil and cook over medium heat until browned, about 10 minutes.

Once cooled, store it in the fridge for up to 2 days or in the freezer for up to 3 months in an airtight container or freezer bag. Alternatively, you can freeze the uncooked sausage if you're working with meat that you just harvested (see Note).

NOTE: I wouldn't recommend thawing frozen venison, mixing this up and then freezing it raw again. If you're using older venison, go ahead and brown it and use it within a few days or freeze it precooked.

Kebabs with Tahini-Yogurt Sauce

SERVES 4

GLUTEN FREE | DAIRY FREE

Making kebabs is one of my favorite ways to use up venison. You can cut the meat into chunks, remove the sinew and plop it in a great marinade. This is perfect for less tender leg meat, but it also works great with backstrap or tenderloin. You're going to love the fresh earthiness of the tahini-yogurt sauce! This pairs perfectly with Couscous Salad with Tomatoes & Cucumbers (page 149).

1 lb (455 g) venison (steaks, chops, backstrap or tenderloin)

1 recipe All-Purpose Marinade (page 123)

¼ cup (60 g) tahini

3 tbsp (45 ml) plain Greek yogurt

¼ tsp garlic powder

¼ tsp salt

¼ tsp Italian seasoning

¼ tsp pepper

Juice of ½ lemon

¼ cup (60 ml) water

Cube the venison and place it into a zip-top bag or bowl. Add the marinade, seal the bag or cover the bowl, place it in the fridge and marinate the meat for at least 1 hour or overnight.

When you're ready to cook, preheat a grill pan or a grill to medium-high heat. If you're using wooden skewers, soak them in water until you're ready to use them.

Skewer the venison cubes. Grill the venison for 3 to 4 minutes per side, or until the meat is medium-rare. If you're using a meat thermometer, cook until the meat reaches 125 to 130°F (52 to 54°C).

Let the meat rest while you mix together the tahini, Greek yogurt, garlic powder, salt, Italian seasoning, pepper, lemon juice and water in a bowl.

Scoop the sauce into little dipping bowls and serve the kebabs with the sauce.

Classic Italian Meatballs

SERVES 4 TO 6

GLUTEN FREE | DAIRY FREE

I love these gluten-free, classic meatballs. I always make my meatballs with almond meal because I love the crunch and flavor. And when I eat them with zoodles (zucchini noodles), I can easily have a really nourishing and veggie-packed meal.

These are great for meal prep. I almost always make a double batch because I try to have a batch of these on hand in the freezer for when life gets busy! When freezing them, I bake them off and then freeze them on a baking sheet lined with parchment. Once they're frozen, they get stored in a freezer bag or glass container. Then I plop them in a pot of sauce, still frozen, when I want to eat. See? So simple!

2 tbsp (30 ml) olive oil

1 yellow onion, finely diced

4 cloves garlic, minced

1 tbsp (15 ml) balsamic vinegar or red wine vinegar (balsamic is my favorite)

1 tbsp (5 g) Italian seasoning

1 tsp salt

½ tsp pepper

1 lb (455 g) ground venison

½ lb (226 g) ground pork

1 egg, lightly beaten

¼ cup (25 g) almond meal

Preheat the oven to 375°F (190°C) and line a baking sheet with foil or a Silpat.

Heat the olive oil in a skillet over medium-high heat and add the onion. Sauté for about 4 minutes, then add the garlic, vinegar, Italian seasoning, salt and pepper. Cook until lightly caramelized, 4 to 5 minutes.

Add the onion and garlic mixture (with the oil) to a large bowl along with the venison, pork, egg and almond meal. Mix well (I like to use my hands).

Scoop the meatball mixture into even balls and roll to shape them evenly. I like to use a large cookie scoop with 1½ to 2 tablespoons (22 to 30 g) in each ball. Arrange the meatballs on the baking sheet so they don't touch. Place the meatballs in the oven and bake for 20 to 25 minutes, until they're golden brown and cooked through.

Discard any fat that has rendered off the meatballs. Add them to your favorite sauce or freeze them on a baking sheet and then store in a freezer bag or container to use later.

Barbacoa Meat

Once you make this barbacoa meat, you'll never ever make tacos with ground meat again. You also won't believe this stuff is made out of venison.

Traditional barbacoa is steam cooked in an underground oven. Since I'm betting that most of us don't have underground ovens like they do in Mexico, we'll do a traditional sear and low and slow roast on the meat. It works wonderfully, if I do say so myself. Use this meat in tacos, quesadillas, burritos, egg bakes, bowls, casseroles—really whenever you want pulled meat with a bit more flavor!

2 tbsp (30 ml) olive oil

2½ to 3 lb (1.1 to 1.4 kg) venison roast

1 (6-oz [168-g]) can tomato paste

Juice of 2 oranges

Juice of 2 limes

1 tbsp (15 ml) apple cider vinegar

2 tsp (4 g) chili powder

2 tsp (4 g) ground cumin

1 tsp salt

½ tsp pepper

½ cup (120 ml) beef or venison stock, homemade (page 124) or store-bought

Preheat the oven to 350°F (180°C).

Heat a large Dutch oven or pot over medium-high heat and add the olive oil. When the oil is hot, add the venison and sear it well on all sides, 4 minutes per side. It should be nice and crusty and brown on each side.

When the venison is seared, remove it from the heat and discard the fat and oil in the pot. If you're using a Dutch oven, you can make the barbacoa meat right in it. If not, transfer the meat to a baking dish.

In a bowl, mix together the tomato paste, orange juice, lime juice, vinegar, chili powder, cumin, salt and pepper. Brush the tomato mixture all over the roast.

Pour the stock into the bottom of your cooking vessel, cover it with a lid or foil and bake for 2½ to 3 hours. The roast should pull apart really easily. When it's done, let it cool, then shred the venison with two forks. Mix everything together so it absorbs all the yummy liquid from the pan.

Transfer the meat to a baking sheet, turn the oven to high broil and cook until the edges of the meat are charred, about 5 minutes.

One-Pot Curry

SERVES 4
GLUTEN FREE | DAIRY FREE

I didn't grow up eating many curry-spiced dishes, but as turmeric has made its debut all over the Internet the past few years, I've learned just how much I enjoy curries and Indian food. Curry is a beautiful spice blend to pair with venison. It's really warming and cozy, and this recipe is very healthy. This is another great recipe for using up steaks that have a lot of sinew because the meat is cubed before cooking. The meat is seared and then braised in the curry sauce. I like to serve it over brown rice to soak up all of the goodness.

1 lb (455 g) venison steaks or chops

1 tbsp (15 ml) olive oil

3 cloves garlic, crushed and minced

½" (1.3-cm) piece fresh ginger, grated

1 tbsp (15 ml) white wine vinegar

2 tsp (4 g) curry powder

1 tsp salt

½ tsp pepper

¾ cup (180 ml) beef or venison stock, homemade (page 124) or store-bought

Steamed rice, for serving

Chopped cilantro, for garnish (optional)

Cut the venison into bite-size cubes, making sure to remove any sinew. This helps the meat get really tender.

Heat the oil in a large pot or Dutch oven over medium-high heat. Once the oil is hot, add the cubed venison and brown it all over for 5 to 7 minutes. Turn the heat down to medium, add the garlic and ginger and sauté for 2 minutes. Deglaze the pan with the vinegar, scraping up all the bits from the bottom of the pan, and add the curry powder, salt and pepper. Toast the spices for 2 minutes before deglazing the pan again with the stock.

Turn the heat to low and cover the pot, letting the meat braise in the curry sauce for about 30 minutes, or until the meat is really tender. Serve over rice with plenty of the curry sauce spooned on top. Garnish with cilantro, if desired.

Chimichurri-Marinated Steak with Fresh Salsa

SERVES 4

GLUTEN FREE | DAIRY FREE

Is there anything better than a really well-cooked steak with the tangy and bright flavors of fresh salsa? Specific, yes. Delicious, very much so.

This is a simple recipe to whip up on a warm summer night, or when you're wanting to bring a bit of warm weather inside. My Restaurant-Style Salsa (page 138) is the perfect accompaniment. The steak is marinated in my Chimichurri Marinade (page 128), which tenderizes the meat and provides a punch of flavor.

1 lb (455 g) venison steaks

1 recipe Chimichurri Marinade (page 128)

¼ cup (60 g) Restaurant-Style Salsa (page 138)

Place the steaks in a bowl or a zip-top bag. Add the marinade, cover the bowl or seal the bag and marinate in the fridge for a least 1 hour or up to 4 hours.

When you're ready to grill, remove the steaks from the fridge, remove them from the marinade and let them come to room temperature while you preheat your grill to medium-high heat (if you have a wood pellet grill, preheat to 450°F [230°C]).

Grill the steaks for 3 to 4 minutes per side, or until rare to medium-rare (they should register 125 to 135°F [52 to 58°C] on a meat thermometer). Pull them off the grill and let the steaks rest for 10 minutes before serving with the salsa.

Zucchini Meatball Boats

I love anything in zucchini boat form. These feel really fun because it's kind of like a meatball sub, but if you feel like packing in another serving of veggies, then this is for you! You're going to fall in love with the venison meatballs in here. I try to keep a bag in the freezer at all times.

4 medium-size zucchini

1 tsp olive oil

¼ tsp salt

1 recipe cooked Classic Italian Meatballs (page 44)

2 cups (480 ml) your favorite marinara sauce

¼ cup (25 g) grated Parmesan cheese (optional)

Preheat the oven to 375°F (190°C).

Slice the zucchini in half lengthwise and place them cut side up on a baking sheet. Drizzle the zucchini with the olive oil and sprinkle with the salt. Bake them for 10 minutes, until they start to get soft.

Meanwhile, toss the meatballs in the marinara sauce.

Remove the zucchini halves from the oven and let them cool. Scoop half of the insides out of the center to create a moat for the meatballs and sauce.

Spoon the meatballs and sauce inside the zucchini and top with the Parmesan cheese, if using.

Pop the boats back in the oven for 5 minutes to melt the cheese.

NOTE: You may have a few meatballs leftover. They keep well in the fridge for 2 to 3 days, or for 3 months in the freezer.

Small Plates & Snacks

When people think of venison, they usually think of heavy main dish meals. But, *au contraire*, my friends! I'm going to give you so many ideas for serving wild game for starters and snacks when entertaining, or when you just want to make a small plate or two to switch up your weekend dinner routine.

My favorite part of this chapter has to be the Wild Game Charcuterie Board (page 56), but you'll find ideas for what to serve on it weaved through the whole chapter. This chapter is really just a flavor party, and we're all invited.

Wild Game Charcuterie Board

This recipe is more of an idea center to give you some inspiration when creating charcuterie boards with your wild game meat. This is a great way to use up what you have on hand in a more elevated fashion.

In addition to listing the meats I like to use, I suggest different cheeses, finger foods and accompaniments that go wonderfully with the bold flavors of venison and wild game. I'll walk you through how I set up cheese boards—what to place first, where and why. Pick two or three meats and cheeses from the list (or more if you want) and a few accompaniments and you'll be creating impressive charcuterie boards at home in no time!

MEATS

Easiest Black Pepper Jerky (page 66)

Carpaccio (page 65)

Caramelized Onion & Goat Cheese Crostini (page 62)

Sliced bologna

Any cured wild game meat

CHEESES

Asiago: Italian cow's milk cheese, opt for aged—intense, nutty

Manchego: Spanish sheep's milk cheese—nutty, tangy, fresh

Cheddar: Cow's milk cheese, opt for sharp white—intense, nutty

Parmesan: Italian cow's milk cheese—intense, nutty

Chèvre: Goat's milk cheese—fresh, pungent, tangy (cranberry goat cheese or goat cheese with dried fruit is especially delicious)

Stilton: English cow's milk blue cheese—tangy, pungent

FRESH PRODUCE

Pomegranate arils (one of my favorite cheese board additions)

Apples

Oranges

Blueberries

Huckleberries

Carrots

Peaches

Tomatoes

Beets

Artichokes

DRIED FRUIT (OR CHOCOLATE-COVERED DRIED FRUIT)

Cranberries

Cherries

Blueberries

Raisins

Pomegranate arils

NUTS (HERB-ROASTED NUTS ARE A VERY SMART CHOICE)

Almonds

Cashews

Chestnuts

JARRED GOODS

Cornichons

Pickled ginger

Green olives

Horseradish

Honey

Marinated artichokes

CRACKERS

Look for a variety of nutty crackers, mild crackers and even those little Parmesan crisps

FRESH HERBS (FOR GARNISH)

Rosemary

Thyme

WINE PAIRINGS (OPTIONAL)

Dry, robust red: Cabernet Sauvignon, Mourvedre, Sangiovese, Malbec, Petit Sirah, Bordeaux Blend

Dry, crisp white: Sauvignon Blanc, Grüner Veltliner, Soave, Pinot Gris

Select what you'll be serving on. I like to use my large wooden countertop cutting board if we have more than four in our party.

Lay out the biggest items first. This will most likely be your cheeses and things like a plate of carpaccio or crostini. I like to pick a corner of my board and lay the biggest thing there and then place large items down the diagonal of my surface and in the corners. This creates visually appealing lines.

Once you have your cheese on the board, cut a few slices to get guests started. No one wants to be the first one to cut into something that hasn't been touched yet. Having slices available invites them to dive in. Once a few slices are done, I stick the cheese knives in the cheese so there's no wondering how to cut more.

Then, start to fill in with cured meats. I like to cut cured meats for my guests. It can be tricky and awkward to do with an appetizer plate in your hand.

Next, fill in with the crackers. You can see we're working from largest to smallest. Fill in the rest of the board with any other accompaniments you might have and fill any last spaces with herbs.

If you're setting out wine, do so and get ready to dig in!

*See photo on page 54.

Mediterranean Nachos

Mediterranean nachos are an appetizer I like to bust out when the weather gets warm for a little something different. I've gotten some questionable looks when I've carried out a platter of pita chips piled high with ground meat, tzatziki and veggies, but the trepidation quickly goes away after the first bite.

This is one of those crowd-pleasing appetizers that's simple to whip up any time of year; it doesn't have to be hot outside. The tomatoes and cucumbers even make it festive enough for the holidays!

1 tbsp (15 ml) olive oil

1 lb (455 g) ground venison

1 tsp red wine vinegar

2 tsp (5 g) garlic powder, divided

1½ tsp (7 g) salt, divided

1 tsp pepper, divided

1 cup (240 ml) plain Greek yogurt (I like full fat)

3 tbsp (45 ml) water

Juice of 1 lemon

1 tbsp (4 g) chopped fresh dill

1 tsp honey

2 (8-oz [226-g]) bags pita chips

1 cucumber, diced

3 Roma tomatoes, diced

½ cup (75 g) crumbled feta cheese

Heat the olive oil in a large skillet over medium heat. Add the venison and cook, stirring occasionally, until the venison is browned, about 8 minutes.

Add the vinegar, 1 teaspoon of the garlic powder, ½ teaspoon of the salt and ½ teaspoon of the pepper. Cook for 2 more minutes, and then remove the skillet from the heat. Set the meat aside.

To make the tzatziki drizzle, mix together the Greek yogurt, water, lemon juice, dill, honey, remaining 1 teaspoon of garlic powder, remaining 1 teaspoon of salt and remaining ½ teaspoon of pepper.

To assemble the nachos, lay down a layer of the pita chips and pile them high with the ground venison, cucumber and tomatoes. Drizzle on the tzatziki sauce and sprinkle on the feta cheese.

Asian Lettuce Wraps

I love ordering lettuce cups as a starter or light entrée when I'm out to eat. They're so fresh and flavorful. It's those smoky, bright and tangy flavors that always make me want to come back for more.

This is another great appetizer (or small plate) to whip up when you're entertaining, for those who don't regularly eat wild game. The spices really transform the flavor of the venison; I bet no one would even guess it was deer meat if you didn't tell them!

1 tbsp (15 ml) olive or coconut oil

1 lb (455 g) ground venison

3 tbsp (45 ml) soy sauce (or coconut aminos for soy/gluten free)

1 tbsp (15 ml) hoisin sauce

1 tbsp (15 ml) rice wine vinegar or white wine vinegar

1 tsp Chinese five-spice powder

½ tsp garlic powder

¼ tsp ground ginger

½ cup (50 g) chopped water chestnuts

1 head butter lettuce

Sriracha, for serving (optional)

Chopped scallion, for serving (optional)

Heat the oil in a large skillet over medium heat. Once the oil is hot, add the venison and cook, stirring occasionally, until the venison is browned, about 8 minutes.

Add the soy sauce, hoisin sauce, vinegar, five-spice powder, garlic powder and ginger. Cook, stirring, until the liquid evaporates, about 5 minutes. Add the water chestnuts and remove the pan from the heat, stirring everything together well.

Lay the butter lettuce leaves out on a plate and fill each with the venison filling. You may want to double up on lettuce for some of the smaller or weaker pieces. If desired, drizzle with sriracha and sprinkle with scallions before serving.

Caramelized Onion & Goat Cheese Crostini

MAKES 12 TO 16 CROSTINI

I love to serve this recipe at a party. It's a little bit fancy, but so gosh darn easy to make. And don't even get me started on the mixture of goat cheese and blue cheese. Even if you're not really a blue cheese person, I encourage you to try this. Start the caramelized onions early, or prep them in advance and this will come together in no time.

One thing to note is that the crostini are best served with medium-rare venison. Cook it to an internal temperature of 120 to 125°F (49 to 52°C). Let it rest for 10 minutes before slicing it into bite-size pieces. The medium-rare preparation and the small pieces will make this easier for guests to bite into—a must for handheld hors d'oeuvres.

2 tbsp (30 g) butter

2 sweet yellow onions, thinly sliced

8 oz (226 g) goat cheese

2 tbsp (19 g) crumbled blue cheese

½ lb (226 g) venison steak (I like to use tenderloin or backstrap)

1 tsp olive oil

Pinch of salt

Pinch of pepper

1 baguette

½ cup (15 g) arugula

2 tbsp (30 ml) balsamic glaze (I buy this premade at the grocery store)

Lemon zest, for garnishing (optional)

Chopped fresh thyme, for garnishing (optional)

Melt the butter in a medium sauté pan over medium-low heat and add the onions. Let the onions caramelize, stirring occasionally, for 30 to 40 minutes. Low and slow is the name of the game here. This can be done up to 2 days ahead of time if you're entertaining.

While the onions caramelize, or when you're ready to assemble, mix together the goat and blue cheeses in a small bowl. Rub the venison with the olive oil, salt and pepper.

Heat a grill pan or skillet over medium-high heat until it's very hot. Sear the venison on both sides and cook it for about 8 minutes total, or until it reaches an internal temperature of 125°F (52°C). Note that you may need less cooking time with a thin piece of meat. Remove it from the heat and tent it with foil to rest for 10 minutes, then cut it into bite-size pieces.

Cut the bread into ½-inch (1.3-cm) slices. Toast in the oven or carefully char it in a pan over high heat.

When the onions have caramelized and the meat has rested, assemble the crostini. Spread a thin layer of the cheese on each bread slice, add some arugula, top with the caramelized onion, pile on some venison and then finish it all with a balsamic drizzle. Garnish with the lemon zest and thyme, if using.

NOTE: If you're feeding a crowd, serve these in store-bought mini phyllo tartlets. Fill the cooked tartlet with the cheese mixture, chop up the arugula and meat and just assemble. This would be great for serving more than 10 people.

Carpaccio

SERVES 4 TO 8

It's important to note that you only want to work with very fresh meat when making carpaccio because it is served raw. This is a dish you would want to make to celebrate right after you harvest a deer. I wouldn't recommend defrosting a piece of meat and preparing this dish.

Now, carpaccio is something I see in upscale steakhouses, but it's insanely simple to do at home. All you have to do is pound the end of a deer tenderloin to a paper-thin thickness and drizzle it with plenty of acid, olive oil, salt and pepper. I like my carpaccio served over arugula and as a part of my Wild Game Charcuterie Board (page 56).

½ lb (226 g) venison tenderloin (cut the end off one of the tenderloins as you're processing the meat)

2 tbsp (30 ml) olive oil

1 tbsp (15 ml) red wine vinegar

Juice of 1 lemon

½ tsp salt

½ tsp freshly ground black pepper, plus more for serving

¼ tsp sugar

Arugula, for serving (optional)

Freshly grated Parmesan cheese, for serving (optional)

Wrap the tenderloin piece tightly in plastic wrap and freeze it for 2 hours. This makes it easier to slice the meat thinly. Freezing raw meat also helps kill bacteria, making it safer to eat.

When the 2 hours have passed, slice the meat as thinly as you can. Place each slice between two pieces of parchment paper or plastic wrap and pound until paper-thin.

In a bowl, whisk together the olive oil, vinegar, lemon juice, salt, pepper and sugar.

Lay the slices of tenderloin over a bed of arugula (if using) and drizzle the vinaigrette all over the meat. Top with more pepper and Parmesan cheese (if using). Chill for a few hours or serve immediately. Only consume this the day you make it.

Easiest Black Pepper Jerky

I love jerky. It's kind of my favorite gas station indulgence. But . . . yeah, the ingredients aren't so awesome, and I definitely prefer venison over beef because it's much less fatty. I prefer dry, chewy jerky, and I know a lot of people do, too.

The trick to jerky is a really lean cut of meat. Flank steak works best; alternatives are some pieces of the foreleg or a super lean sirloin. I like to pound pieces out until they're really thin, too. My preferred method for making jerky is with a dehydrator. You can make jerky in the oven, but the dehydrator produces the best jerky with less room for error.

1 lb (455 g) venison flank steak (or another lean cut like a foreleg steak)

¼ cup (60 ml) soy sauce (or coconut aminos for soy/gluten free)

About 10 dashes Worcestershire sauce

2 tsp (4 g) freshly ground black pepper

Slice the steak into strips or chunks, whatever shape of jerky you desire. I like rectangular pieces. If needed, pound out the pieces to be about ¼ inch (6 mm) thick.

Add the jerky strips to a bowl or zip-top bag and add the soy sauce, Worcestershire sauce and black pepper. Toss well to coat. Cover the bowl or seal the bag and marinate the jerky in the fridge for at least 8 hours, or up to 48 hours. I like at least 24 hours for lots of savory, black pepper flavor!

DEHYDRATOR INSTRUCTIONS (MY PREFERRED METHOD): Arrange the jerky in one flat layer on the tray. Set the dehydrator to 155°F (68°C) and place the tray in the dehydrator. Let the jerky dehydrate for 4 hours, or until it is totally dry.

OVEN INSTRUCTIONS: Preheat the oven to 155°F (68°C). Set a drying rack on a baking sheet to let air circulate all around the jerky. Place the jerky slices in an even layer on the drying rack and let the jerky dry out in the oven for about 4 hours, checking frequently to make sure that it's not too dry and brittle.

Store the jerky in an airtight container in the fridge for up to 1 month.

Crispy Chorizo Brussels Sprouts with Sriracha-Honey Sauce

SERVES 4 TO 6
GLUTEN FREE |
DAIRY FREE

I love finding Brussels sprouts on menus as a starter, especially when they're roasted until crispy. I easily get tired of heavy and greasy appetizers—by the time you get to the main dish, you're too full to enjoy what you've ordered.

I love to serve this hot out of the oven as an appetizer to set out on the counter, or as a side dish. It has my favorite venison chorizo AND an addicting sriracha-honey glaze. Tons of flavor for a lighter and creative starter.

1 lb (455 g) Brussels sprouts, halved

2 tsp (10 ml) olive oil

¾ tsp salt, divided

¼ tsp pepper

½ cup (120 g) cooked Venison Chorizo (page 39)

Juice of 1 lemon

1 tbsp (15 ml) sriracha

2 tsp (10 ml) honey

¼ tsp garlic powder

Preheat the oven to 400°F (200°C).

Spread the Brussels sprouts on a baking sheet, drizzle them with the olive oil, sprinkle them with ½ teaspoon of the salt and the pepper and roast them for 20 minutes, or until they're crispy around the edges. Add the chorizo to the pan and pop it back into the oven for 5 minutes. This will heat the chorizo.

In a bowl, whisk together the lemon juice, sriracha, honey, garlic powder and remaining ¼ teaspoon of salt.

When the Brussels sprouts are crispy and the chorizo is warmed through, drizzle with the sauce and toss everything together. Serve hot!

Flatbread with Meatballs & Balsamic

Flatbread is such an easy starter or a small meal, and I often don't think to make it at home. All you need is some good flatbread (or naan works beautifully) and a few toppings. Here, I love to lay down a base of mozzarella, add some arugula, pile on some meatballs and top it all off with a balsamic drizzle. All in all, it's a five-ingredient recipe that's really impressive and fast. It's very festive for the holidays!

1 flatbread or naan

4 oz (112 g) shredded mozzarella

1 handful arugula

4 cooked Classic Italian Meatballs (page 44)

2 tbsp (30 ml) balsamic glaze (I buy this premade at the grocery store)

Preheat the oven to 450°F (230°C).

Place the flatbread on a baking sheet and cover it with the mozzarella cheese. Lay the arugula all over the cheese. I like to halve the meatballs and lay them all over the flatbread, but you could leave them whole or even crumble them. That's up to you.

Bake for 8 to 12 minutes, or until the cheese is melted and the meatballs are heated through.

Remove it from the oven and drizzle it all over with the balsamic glaze. Slice it with a pizza cutter and serve!

Chorizo Sweet Potato Nachos

SERVES 2 FOR DINNER,
4 TO 6 FOR AN APPETIZER
GLUTEN FREE

The first time I made these I popped them out of the oven, all melty and gooey, piled on the toppings, and set the pan right smack dab in the middle of our kitchen island. Jared kindly asked me if I wanted him to set the table and I insisted that we pull up some barstools and eat right out of the pan. It was wonderful.

There's enough here for two to share for a cozy dinner, or make it for a small party as an appetizer. You could easily double or triple the recipe for a crowd.

2 large or 3 medium sweet potatoes, peeled and sliced into ¼" (6-mm) rounds

2 tsp (10 ml) olive oil

½ tsp salt

¼ tsp black pepper

1 cup (240 g) cooked Venison Chorizo (page 39)

1 cup (113 g) shredded pepper Jack cheese

OPTIONAL TOPPINGS

Sour cream

Sliced tomatoes

Sliced jalapeño peppers

Sliced avocado

Black beans

Chopped fresh cilantro

Minced red onion

Preheat the oven to 400°F (200°C).

Spread the sweet potato slices evenly on two baking sheets so they are all in one flat layer. Drizzle on the olive oil and sprinkle with the salt and pepper. Massage the oil and seasonings all over the slices, then spread them in a single layer again.

Pop the baking sheets into the oven and bake for 15 minutes, flipping the slices halfway through. The sweet potatoes should be lightly browned and soft in the middle. Remove them from the oven and let them cool slightly so you can handle them.

Either in an ovenproof skillet or on one of the baking sheets, spread half of the sweet potatoes in an even layer. Sprinkle on half of the chorizo and half of the cheese. Pile on the remaining half of the sweet potatoes, chorizo and cheese.

Place the pan or skillet back into the oven and bake for 5 minutes, or until the cheese is melted.

Remove the nachos from the oven and top with your desired toppings. Dig in! This is best eaten hot out of the oven.

Cranberry-Orange Party Meatballs

This is the perfect appetizer to serve in the fall and winter. The bright and tangy flavors of cranberry and orange marry together beautifully and do some pretty wonderful things to the venison. This is one of those things you can serve to unsuspecting guests, and they won't even know they're eating wild game.

This is a slow cooker recipe, as it's the easiest way to do it. Or you can dump all of the sauce ingredients into a saucepan, warm and pour over the cooked meatballs, if you'd prefer.

FOR THE MEATBALLS

1 lb (455 g) ground venison

½ lb (226 g) ground pork

1 onion, minced

Juice of ½ lemon

1 tsp Dijon mustard

2 tsp (8 g) coconut sugar

1 tsp salt

1 tsp garlic powder

½ tsp pepper

Pinch of nutmeg

1 egg, beaten

¼ cup (25 g) almond meal or bread crumbs

FOR THE CRANBERRY-ORANGE SAUCE

1 small onion, minced

1 (15-oz [420-g]) can whole cranberry sauce

2 cloves garlic, minced

¼ cup (60 ml) maple syrup

1 (6-oz [168-g]) can tomato paste

Juice and zest of 1 orange

1 tsp red chile paste

1 tsp chili powder

1 tsp salt

To make the meatballs, preheat the oven to 400°F (200°C) and line a baking sheet with foil or a Silpat.

Add all of the ingredients for the meatballs to a large bowl and mix until everything is well incorporated. I like to do this with my hands and a fork.

Using a large cookie scoop, scoop balls of the meatball mixture and roll between your hands to make them evenly shaped. Place them on the prepared baking sheet. Bake the meatballs for 18 minutes, then remove them from the oven and set them aside.

To make the sauce, add all of the sauce ingredients to the insert of a slow cooker. Mix everything together well. Add the cooked meatballs and fold them into the sauce until they are all covered.

Turn the slow cooker to high and cook for 2 hours to warm the sauce to perfection.

To serve, turn the slow cooker to warm and set out some toothpicks and let everyone go to town!

Jalapeño Poppers

I always get excited when I see jalapeño poppers on a menu. I love the creamy inside contrasted with the crunchy, spicy, fresh pepper. I prefer mine with meat in the middle, not just cream cheese and cheese. Too much cheese overpowers it for me; it's very rich. You're going to love the addition of venison here. With a squeeze of fresh lime, these are little bites of heaven.

1 tsp olive oil

½ lb (226 g) ground venison

4 oz (112 g) cream cheese, softened

Juice of ½ lime

½ tsp garlic powder

¾ tsp salt

¾ cup (84 g) shredded pepper Jack cheese, divided

12 jalapeño peppers, halved and seeded (see Notes)

Preheat the oven to 375°F (190°C). Line a baking sheet with parchment paper.

Warm the olive oil in a skillet over medium heat. Add the venison and cook, stirring occasionally, until it is browned and cooked through, about 8 minutes. Transfer to a medium-size mixing bowl. Add the cream cheese, lime juice, garlic powder, salt and ½ cup (57 g) of the cheese and mix well.

Place the jalapeño halves on the prepared baking sheet and stuff them with the venison cream cheese mixture. Sprinkle the remaining ¼ cup (27 g) of cheese on top.

Bake for 10 minutes, then turn the oven to low broil and move the baking sheet to the top rack of the oven. Broil for 3 to 5 minutes, watching carefully so that the cheese doesn't burn, and cook until the cheese is golden and bubbly. Serve immediately.

NOTES: Be careful when seeding jalapeños. You may want to wear kitchen gloves, as the oils from the jalapeños can burn the skin and eyes.

These are also wonderful made on a wood pellet grill or smoker—the kiss of smoky flavor is delicious. Finish them under the broiler before serving, if desired.

Lightened-Up Taco Dip

Oh, how I love taco dip! There are so many ways to do it, but I like mine heavy on the meat, salsa and cream cheese. Oh, and piled high with crunchy, fresh veggies, too! This is the perfect thing to set out for a party or to bring to one. (Psst, no one will even know you're serving them wild game.)

1 tbsp (15 ml) olive oil

1 small yellow onion, finely diced (about 1 cup [160 g])

1 lb (455 g) ground venison

1 tsp chili powder

½ tsp garlic powder

1 tsp salt, divided

¼ tsp black pepper

Juice of 1 lime, divided

2 cups (480 ml) plain Greek yogurt (I like full fat)

8 oz (226 g) cream cheese, softened

½ cup (120 g) salsa, homemade (page 138) or store-bought

2 cups (60 g) shredded or finely chopped lettuce

2 Roma tomatoes, diced

1½ cups (170 g) shredded pepper Jack cheese

1 jalapeño pepper, sliced (optional)

Chips or veggies, for serving

Heat the olive oil in a large skillet over medium heat. Add the onion and sauté for 3 to 5 minutes, until golden and translucent. Add the venison and cook, stirring occasionally, until the venison is browned, about 8 minutes.

Add the chili powder, garlic powder, ½ teaspoon of the salt, pepper and half the lime juice. Cook for 2 more minutes, stirring, to let the spices release their flavor, and then remove the skillet from the heat.

In a medium-size bowl, combine the Greek yogurt, cream cheese, salsa, the remaining half of the lime juice and the remaining ½ teaspoon of salt. Spread the creamy yogurt layer onto the bottom of a 9 x 13–inch (23 x 33–cm) pan. Sprinkle the venison mixture over the yogurt layer. Top with the lettuce, tomatoes, cheese and jalapeño, if using.

Serve the dip right away with chips or refrigerate it, covered, for a few hours.

Soups & Salads

I could eat soup and salad for almost every meal, any time of the year. Venison is absolutely perfect for soup, and I like to make big batches of each of these to have on hand during the colder months. They all freeze beautifully.

Creative salads are a great, healthy way to use up deer meat. You won't believe how simple these are to throw together for quick lunches and dinners!

A lot of these recipes are inspired by dishes I find myself ordering when I'm out to eat, especially at our favorite local Italian joint. I love re-creating my favorite meals at home.

Italian Wedding Soup

SERVES 8 TO 10
DAIRY FREE

Our favorite Italian restaurant has Italian wedding soup on the menu every Sunday. And it's absolutely glorious. So, you know I had to make my own with venison! The Italian Sausage recipe (page 40) makes the best little meatballs for this recipe. Comfort food at its finest, folks.

This makes a big batch. What I usually do is freeze half of it into one- or two-person servings for grab-and-go weekend lunches.

1 recipe uncooked Italian Sausage (page 40)

1 tbsp (15 ml) olive oil

1 large yellow onion, diced

1½ cups (192 g) diced carrot

3 cloves garlic, minced

1 tbsp (6 g) Italian seasoning

1 tsp salt

¼ tsp pepper

8 cups (1.9 L) low-sodium chicken broth

1 (16-oz [455-g]) box acini de pepe pasta, cooked according to package directions

1 tsp lemon juice, or more to taste

4 cups (120 g) spinach

Preheat the oven to 400°F (200°C). Line a baking sheet with foil or a Silpat.

Shape the sausage mixture into small meatballs using a small cookie scoop or about 2 teaspoons (10 g) of meat per meatball. Place the meatballs on the prepared baking sheet and bake for 10 to 12 minutes, until they're cooked through and browned.

While the meatballs cook, start on the soup. Heat the olive oil in a large pot over medium heat. Add the onion and carrot and cook for 5 minutes. Add the garlic, Italian seasoning, salt and pepper and cook for 2 minutes longer. Add the chicken broth and heat through.

When the meatballs have finished cooking, add them to the pot and bring the soup to a boil. Lower the heat, cover the pot and simmer for 20 minutes, then add the cooked pasta, lemon juice and spinach. Remove from the heat, stir and serve hot!

Spicy Chipotle Chocolate Chili

I know what you're thinking: "Another deer chili recipe? Come on!" But it honestly almost felt wrong to write this book without a chili recipe included. So, I decided to elevate your experience.

We've got the usual suspects here, but we're also folding in elements of richness with smoky chipotles and decadent Mexican (or unsweetened) chocolate. I chose to balance the chocolate with lots of fresh lime juice and light-bodied beer. A lot of times I use dark beer in my chili, but not with this recipe. Spice lovers rejoice—this one has a good bit of smoldering heat that creeps up on you, but you can dial that down by eliminating the jalapeño if you want.

1 tbsp (15 ml) olive oil

1 onion, diced

1 green bell pepper, cored and diced

1 yellow or red bell pepper, cored and diced

1 jalapeño pepper, diced (seeded for less heat)

3 cloves garlic, minced

1 lb (455 g) ground venison

2 tbsp (12 g) chili powder

1 tbsp (6 g) ground cumin

½ tsp ground cinnamon

Juice of 2 limes

12 oz (360 ml) light-bodied beer (I like Corona, Modelo or Michelob Ultra)

1 oz (28 g) Mexican or unsweetened chocolate, chopped

1 (7-oz [196-g]) can chipotle peppers, with juice

1 (15-oz [420-g]) can black beans, drained and rinsed

1 (15-oz [420-g]) can kidney beans, drained and rinsed

1 (28-oz [784-g]) can diced tomatoes, with juice

Heat the olive oil in a large stockpot or Dutch oven over medium heat. Add the onion, bell peppers and jalapeño and sauté for 5 minutes. Add the garlic and venison and cook, stirring occasionally, until the venison is browned, about 8 minutes.

Add the chili powder, cumin and cinnamon and cook, stirring, for 2 minutes to allow the spices to release their flavor. Add the lime juice and beer and deglaze the pan, scraping up all the bits from the bottom of the pan, and cook for 5 minutes, stirring frequently to cook the alcohol out of the beer.

Add the chocolate, chipotles with their juice, black beans, kidney beans and tomatoes with their juice. Mix well and try to break apart the chipotles with your spoon or spatula. Can you smell the flavor?!

Bring the chili to a boil, reduce the heat to low and allow the chili to simmer, covered, for about 20 minutes, or as long as a few hours. Serve hot as is or with your favorite chili fixings.

Pasta Fagioli

SERVES 6 TO 8
DAIRY-FREE OPTION

I had been wanting to make my own version of pasta fagioli for quite some time, and I thought it would be the perfect thing to make with venison. I made sure to add plenty of red wine vinegar to the meat while sautéing it to add some acid, which I strongly feel that venison needs. If I had to, I think I'd pick this venison version over my restaurant fave. It's delicious.

8 oz (226 g) ditalini pasta

1 to 2 tbsp (15 to 30 ml) olive oil

1 onion, diced

1 cup (128 g) diced carrot

1 cup (101 g) diced celery

3 cloves garlic, minced

1 lb (455 g) ground venison

1 tbsp (6 g) Italian seasoning

½ tsp crushed red pepper flakes, plus more for serving (optional)

1 tsp salt

½ tsp black pepper

3 tbsp (45 ml) red wine vinegar

1 (15-oz [420-g]) can cannellini beans, drained and rinsed

1 (15-oz [420-g]) can kidney beans, drained and rinsed

1 (15-oz [420-g]) can tomato sauce

4 cups (960 ml) chicken broth

1 cup (240 ml) reserved pasta water

Grated Parmesan cheese, for serving (optional, omit for dairy free)

Cook the ditalini according to the package directions until al dente, about 10 minutes. Before you drain the pasta, reserve about 1 cup (240 ml) of the pasta water to add to the dish if needed.

Meanwhile, warm the olive oil in a large pot over medium heat. Add the onion, carrot and celery and cook for 5 minutes. Add the garlic and venison and cook, stirring occasionally, until the venison is browned, about 8 minutes.

Add the Italian seasoning, red pepper flakes (if using), salt, pepper and red wine vinegar and cook for 2 minutes longer. Add the beans, tomato sauce and chicken broth. Bring the mixture to a boil, lower the heat and simmer for 20 minutes.

Add the cooked pasta and stir to incorporate. If the mixture is looking a little thick, add some of the reserved pasta water and let it simmer for about 5 minutes to incorporate.

Serve while hot in a big bowl with plenty of Parmesan cheese and red pepper flakes, if desired.

Tuscan White Bean, Kale & Sausage Soup

SERVES 6 TO 8

GLUTEN FREE | DAIRY-FREE OPTION | 30 MINUTES OR LESS

I hate playing favorites, but this is what I think of when I think of the ultimate comfort food. I love that this soup is so hearty and flavorful, but on a day when I'm not feeling my best, the extra servings of veggies from the peppers, tomatoes and kale gets me back on my feet quicker than ever.

I remember when I was in Italy a few years back how few vegetables we ate until we went to Tuscany. There, my family and I had a private meal at a winery with organic produce grown by local monks. I remember sitting there with curly kale and butter lettuce all over my plate as I picked up and ate the leaves with a drizzle of olive oil and sea salt. I felt whole again.

1 tbsp (15 ml) olive oil

1 onion, diced

1 green bell pepper, cored and diced

2 cloves garlic, minced

1 lb (455 g) uncooked Italian Sausage (page 40)

¾ tsp salt, or to taste

½ tsp black pepper

2 tsp (4 g) Italian seasoning

1 tbsp (15 ml) white wine vinegar

2 (15-oz [420-g]) cans cannellini beans, undrained

1 (15-oz [420-g]) can diced tomatoes, with juice

4 cups (960 ml) chicken stock or bone broth

4 cups (268 g) chopped kale

Lemon juice, to taste

Crushed red pepper flakes, for serving (optional)

Grated Parmesan cheese, for serving (optional, omit for dairy free)

Warm the olive oil in a large pot or Dutch oven over medium heat. Add the onion and bell pepper and sauté until soft, 6 to 8 minutes. Add the garlic and Italian sausage and cook, breaking it up into bite-size chunks, until the sausage is browned, about 8 to 10 minutes.

Add the salt, pepper and Italian seasoning and cook for 1 minute. Add the vinegar and deglaze the pan, scraping up any brown bits form the bottom of the pot, and then add the beans with their liquid, tomatoes with their juice and broth. Bring the soup to a boil, decrease the heat to low and simmer for at least 10 minutes.

If you want to eat right away, remove the soup from the heat. Or, let the soup simmer with the lid on for more flavor until you're ready to eat.

When you're ready to serve, stir in the kale and squeeze in the lemon juice. You want to make sure you only add the kale just before serving so it doesn't get mushy. Serve hot with red pepper flakes and Parmesan cheese, if desired.

Asian Chop Salad

SERVES 2 TO 4

GLUTEN FREE | DAIRY FREE | 30 MINUTES OR LESS

This is the perfect healthy recipe for when you're sick of the same ol' boring salad, but you need something quick. It's mega flavorful with notes from the Chinese five-spice powder, soy sauce, hoisin sauce and mandarin oranges. The shredded carrot, cabbage and slivered almonds give the best crunch.

I find the five-spice in the baking and spice section of my grocery store (or online) and the hoisin and rice wine vinegar in the ethnic aisles. I use these ingredients in a couple of other recipes (Asian Lettuce Wraps, page 61, and the Five-Spice Marinade, page 132) in the book and have found them to be great staples in wild game cooking with flair.

FOR THE SALAD

1 tbsp (15 ml) olive oil

1 lb (455 g) ground venison

3 tbsp (45 ml) soy sauce (or coconut aminos for soy/gluten free)

1 tbsp (15 ml) hoisin sauce

1 tbsp (15 ml) rice wine vinegar or white wine vinegar

1 tsp Chinese five-spice powder

½ tsp garlic powder

¼ tsp ground ginger

6 cups (180 g) lettuce

1 cup (70 g) chopped red cabbage

2 large carrots, shredded

8 oz (226 g) mandarin orange slices

½ cup (54 g) slivered almonds

FOR THE DRESSING

2 tbsp (30 ml) olive oil

2 tbsp (30 ml) rice wine vinegar or white wine vinegar

1 tbsp (15 ml) soy sauce (or coconut aminos for soy/gluten free)

1 tsp sriracha

1 tsp hoisin sauce

½ tsp minced garlic

¼ tsp ground ginger

To make the salad, heat the oil in a large skillet over medium heat, add the venison and cook, stirring occasionally, until the venison is browned, about 8 minutes. Add the soy sauce, hoisin sauce, vinegar, five-spice powder, garlic powder and ginger. Mix everything together in the skillet, and let it cook for 5 more minutes to let the flavors get nice and toasty. Remove from the heat and set aside.

While you're cooking the meat, you can chop and shred the veggies for the salad. If it's just me and Jared eating this for a meal, I'll divide the lettuce between two large bowls. If I'm serving to a crowd as a side, I'll add everything to a large bowl. Top the lettuce with the cabbage, carrots, oranges and almonds. Top with the venison when you're ready to serve.

To whip up the dressing quickly, add all of the ingredients to a glass jar with a lid and shake, shake, shake! Pour over the salad and serve.

Herby Mediterranean Pita Salad

SERVES 4
DAIRY FREE

My love for Mediterranean flavors runs deep. This is one of the go-to weeknight meals that I can throw together and use up a lot of different cuts of venison. It features my All-Purpose Marinade (page 123), which tenderizes and adds so much wonderful flavor to the meat. The fresh herbs, pita and hummus really take this dish to the next level!

1 lb (455 g) venison steaks, chops, backstrap or tenderloin

1 recipe All-Purpose Marinade (page 123)

2 pitas

2 tsp (10 ml) plus 3 tbsp (45 ml) olive oil, divided

1 tsp salt, divided

½ tsp garlic powder

6 to 8 cups greens (I use chopped romaine or spring mix)

2 cups (298 g) cherry tomatoes, halved

1 seedless English cucumber, diced

2 tbsp (8 g) chopped fresh oregano

1 tbsp (6 g) chopped fresh mint

3 tbsp (45 ml) red wine vinegar

1 tsp lemon juice

½ tsp pepper

½ cup (120 g) hummus of choice

Cut the venison into bite-size cubes and place in a zip-top bag or large bowl. Add the marinade and stir to coat the meat. Seal the bag or cover the bowl and marinate in the fridge for at least 1 hour or overnight.

When you're ready to cook, preheat the oven to 400°F (200°C).

Heat a large skillet over medium-high, add the venison and cook, stirring occasionally, until medium-rare, 8 to 10 minutes.

While the venison cooks, slice each pita into 4 triangles. Lay them on a baking sheet, drizzle with 2 teaspoons (10 ml) of the olive oil and sprinkle with ½ teaspoon of the salt and the garlic powder. Bake for 10 to 15 minutes, until they're warm and toasty. Set aside until it's time to serve.

Add the mixed greens to a large bowl or divide among four bowls. Top with the tomatoes, cucumber, oregano and mint.

In a small bowl, whisk together the vinegar, lemon juice, remaining 3 tablespoons (45 ml) of olive oil, remaining ½ teaspoon of salt and the pepper. Pour the dressing over the vegetables and toss to coat.

Once the venison and pitas are finished cooking, lay them over the vegetables and add a generous dollop of hummus.

Steak & Blue Cheese Salad

SERVES 4

GLUTEN FREE | 30 MINUTES OR LESS

I have to be in the mood to eat blue cheese on its own, but when it's paired with something meaty like venison medallions, and something sweet like cranberries, I'm in. The pecans provide the perfect nutty addition.

It's best to use a good cut of meat here that's from a tenderloin or backstrap because there's not much done to the meat besides searing it. You also want to make sure you're not cooking it past medium-rare or it's going to get tough. But besides that, this is an easy meal you can whip up in a flash!

FOR THE SALAD

1 lb (455 g) venison tenderloin

1 tbsp (15 ml) olive oil

1 tsp salt

¾ tsp pepper

8 cups (240 g) mixed green lettuce

2 cups (298 g) cherry tomatoes, halved

1 cup (133 g) chopped cucumber

¾ cup (82 g) pecan halves (toasted if you like)

½ cup (61 g) dried cranberries

½ cup (75 g) crumbled blue cheese

FOR THE BALSAMIC DRESSING

¼ cup (60 ml) olive oil

3 tbsp (45 ml) balsamic vinegar

1 tbsp (15 ml) honey

½ tsp salt

½ tsp pepper

To make the salad, remove the venison from the fridge and let it come to room temperature to ensure even cooking; this takes about 30 minutes.

Heat the olive oil in a large skillet over medium-high heat. Sprinkle the salt and pepper all over the venison liberally. Add the venison to the pan and cook for 2 to 3 minutes per side, until medium-rare. If you're using a meat thermometer, it should register 125 to 130°F (52 to 54°C). Immediately remove the venison from the pan and let them rest on a plate while you assemble the salad.

Add the lettuce to a large serving bowl or divide among four bowls. Top with the tomatoes, cucumber, pecans, cranberries and blue cheese.

To make the dressing, in a jar with a lid or in a bowl, add the dressing ingredients and shake or whisk together.

When you're ready to eat, slice the steak against the grain into strips and place on top of the salad. Pour on the dressing and serve.

Breakfast Ideas

Admittedly, breakfast isn't my favorite meal of the day. But, over the years, I've found that there are plenty of breakfast ideas that are great when wild game is used. Not to mention that you're getting lean, free-range protein in your system first thing in the morning.

There are a variety of breakfasts in this chapter—everything from healthy egg cups you can freeze for busy mornings to decadent sausage gravy to pour over biscuits on those mornings when you have a little bit more time. Even if you aren't a big breakfast fan like me, you'll find something you love.

Rustic Breakfast Strata with Greens

Strata is traditionally made with leftover bread, potentially some breakfast meat and vegetables cooked in an egg mixture. It's so divine, even my non-egg-eating husband will scarf down a serving. What I love about strata is that it is really customizable. Have some leftover tomatoes or broccoli from the night before? Toss them in. Or use your favorite bread or cheese— whatever you want, really! The Italian Sausage (page 40) in here is the real winner, though. This is an easy thing to serve the morning after a big meal when you have company in town. Just throw in what you have left over from the night before and you're all set!

12 eggs

1 tbsp (15 ml) milk (we like whole milk)

1 tsp salt

½ tsp pepper

½ tsp garlic powder

1 lb (455 g) cooked Italian Sausage (page 40)

4 cups (400 g) cubed bread (I like sourdough, day old is fine)

¾ cup (85 g) mild, creamy grated cheese like fontina or Gruyère

1 heaping cup (30 g) spinach

1 heaping cup (67 g) kale

Preheat the oven to 350°F (180°C) and grease a 9 x 13–inch (23 x 33–cm) baking dish.

Crack all of the eggs into a large bowl and add the milk, salt, pepper and garlic powder. Whisk until everything is very well combined. Fold in the sausage, bread cubes, cheese, spinach and kale.

Pour the egg and bread mixture into the prepared baking dish and bake for about 40 minutes, or until the egg looks set in the middle and the top is slightly browned. If the bread starts to burn at the edges, just cover the whole dish with foil and bake until the strata is set.

Let it cool for about 10 minutes before slicing and serving up hot!

Huevos Rancheros

Jared and I honeymooned in Jackson Hole, Wyoming, and the food was incredible. One morning, before heading out for a big hike, we went for breakfast, and I ordered a giant plate of huevos rancheros. I cannot even tell you how wonderful that meal was. The flavors were explosive, and Jared, who does not eat eggs, tried AND enjoyed a bite. We've talked about how glorious that breakfast was time and time again, so I thought I'd re-create it at home — with venison, of course.

1 (15-oz [420-g]) can black beans, drained and rinsed

1 tsp lime juice

½ tsp salt

¼ tsp garlic powder

4 tortillas (use corn for gluten free)

½ cup (58 g) shredded Colby Jack cheese

4 eggs

½ cup (120 g) cooked Venison Chorizo (page 39)

OPTIONAL TOPPINGS

Restaurant-Style Salsa (page 138)

Chopped cilantro

Crumbled cotija cheese

Pickled Red Onion (page 150)

Lime quarters

Start by making the black bean spread that goes under and on top of the charred tortilla. Add the black beans, lime juice, salt and garlic powder to a small food processor and whirl it around until it's slightly smooth. You can also mash it with a fork. You want it to be the consistency of chunky peanut butter. Spread about 2 tablespoons (30 g) of the black bean spread on each of four plates (preferably ceramic/microwave safe—you'll see why).

Carefully char the tortillas. I do this over an open flame on my stove, but you could also use the broiler. Watch them closely, because they can burn in an instant. Lay the charred tortillas on top of the black bean spread and spread 1 to 2 tablespoons (15 to 30 g) more of the black beans on top of the tortillas.

Sprinkle the cheese on top of the tortillas, evenly dividing it among the plates. Place the plates in the oven on the middle rack and turn the broiler on low. Broil until the cheese is melted. Carefully remove the plates from the oven; they will be hot.

While the plates are in the oven, grease a skillet, set it over medium-low heat and crack the eggs in. Cook until the whites are cooked and the yolks are runny (sunny side up/fried). Slide the eggs on top of the tortillas when the plates come out of the oven.

If you're using chorizo that has been premade, you may want to warm it in the skillet you cooked the eggs in for a minute or two. Once it's warm, sprinkle it over the eggs. Finish the dish with the toppings of your choice.

NOTE: This recipe can be altered to serve as many or as few people as you want. Just adjust the amounts as necessary (I often make it just for me!).

Blueberry Sage Breakfast Sausage

MAKES ABOUT 14 PATTIES

GLUTEN FREE | DAIRY FREE |
30 MINUTES OR LESS

I like to make my husband healthy breakfast sausage patties for easy mornings. That way, he can just heat something up in a skillet while I'm making myself some eggs. What I normally do is cook these up and then freeze the leftovers on a sheet pan. Once the patties are frozen, I transfer them to a freezer bag, and then we can heat up however many we want when we need them. It's like the healthy, homemade version of Jimmy Dean sausages!

1 lb (455 g) ground venison

1 lb (455 g) ground pork

4 or 5 fresh sage leaves

1 tbsp (15 ml) balsamic vinegar

1 tsp garlic powder

1 tsp onion powder

1 tsp salt

½ tsp pepper

Pinch of ground cinnamon (optional)

½ cup (74 g) blueberries

1 tbsp (15 ml) olive oil

Add the venison, pork, sage, balsamic, garlic powder, onion powder, salt, pepper and cinnamon (if using) to a food processor and process everything for 20 to 30 seconds, until the mixture is relatively smooth. (If you don't have a food processor, use a large bowl and smash everything together with a fork or your hands.) Scrape down the sides of the food processor and add the blueberries. Pulse once or twice to incorporate the blueberries without totally breaking them down. If you're doing this by hand, just mix them in.

To cook the sausages, heat a skillet over medium heat. When it's hot, add the oil. Shape the sausage mixture into patties using 2 to 3 tablespoons (30 to 45 g) per patty. Fry the patties for about 5 minutes per side, or until the sausage is cooked through and browned all over.

Serve them immediately or freeze for up to 3 months. When you're ready to heat them, microwave them in 30-second intervals until hot or cook them on the stovetop in a greased skillet.

Cheesy Hash Brown Bake

SERVES 6
GLUTEN FREE

There's nothing like having a premade breakfast casserole ready for when you have guests. All you have to do is set out some fruit and yogurt and you've got a complete breakfast in a flash. This dish uses ground venison meat, frozen hash browns (an easy, fuss-free ingredient), cheese and a few spices and seasonings. That's it! This is a recipe that even picky eaters will fall for.

1 tbsp (15 g) butter

½ lb (226 g) ground venison

2 tsp (8 g) coconut sugar

1½ tsp (9 g) salt, divided

½ tsp pepper, divided

¼ tsp ground sage

¼ tsp garlic powder

1 tbsp (15 ml) apple cider vinegar

6 eggs

½ cup (120 ml) milk

3 cups (360 g) frozen, shredded hash browns

8 oz (226 g) cheddar cheese, grated, divided

Preheat the oven to 350°F (180°C). Grease an 8 x 8–inch (20 x 20–cm) casserole dish.

Melt the butter in a large skillet over medium heat. Add the venison and cook, stirring occasionally, until the venison is browned, about 8 minutes. Add the coconut sugar, ½ teaspoon of the salt, ¼ teaspoon of the pepper, sage, garlic powder and apple cider vinegar. Cook, stirring, for 2 minutes, then remove the pan from the heat.

In a large bowl, whisk together the eggs, milk, remaining 1 teaspoon of salt and remaining ¼ teaspoon of pepper. Add the hash browns (while they're still frozen) and about 6 ounces (168 g) of the grated cheese. Mix everything together well, and then fold in the venison mixture.

Pour the mixture into the prepared casserole dish and sprinkle the top with the remaining 2 ounces (56 g) of cheese. Cover with foil and bake for 30 minutes; remove the foil and bake for 30 minutes longer. Let the casserole cool for a few minutes before slicing and serving. This can be made 1 to 2 days ahead of time. Store it wrapped tightly in the fridge and heat it up when you want to serve it.

Veggie & Egg Breakfast Bites

MAKES 16 TO 18 CUPS
GLUTEN FREE | DAIRY FREE

If you're in need of a power-packed breakfast, look no further. These veggie and egg cups with ground venison pack a punch and will power you through your day!

I've listed one of my favorite veggie combinations below, but feel free to clean out the fridge and use what you have on hand. Really, any vegetable works. Once baked and cooled, you can store these in the fridge for 2 to 3 days, or freeze them so you can heat them on the go!

1 tbsp (15 ml) olive oil

1 lb (455 g) ground venison

12 eggs

1 large tomato, diced

1 cup (71 g) chopped broccoli

1 tsp Italian seasoning

1 tsp salt

1 tsp pepper

Preheat the oven to 350°F (180°C). Grease 16 to 18 cups of two muffin pans or use silicone muffin pans. Silicone works best.

Heat the olive oil in a large skillet over medium heat. Add the venison and cook, stirring occasionally, until the venison is browned, 8 to 10 minutes.

Meanwhile, whisk the eggs in a large bowl. Add the tomato, broccoli, Italian seasoning, salt and pepper and stir to combine. When the venison has cooked, add the meat to the egg and veggie mixture.

Divide the egg mixture among the prepared muffin cups and bake for about 25 minutes, or until the eggs are completely set.

Scoop or turn them out of the pan and serve. If you want to freeze them, let them cool before freezing on a parchment-lined baking sheet and then you can store them in a freezer bag or container.

Mexican-Style Breakfast Burritos

The hardest meal of the day for me has always been breakfast. I'm so eager to start the day that sometimes I forget to eat! Having these prepped and frozen burritos ready to go is a great solution for a busy morning, or even afternoons during lunchtime. These burritos can be eaten right away, or as I explain below, frozen and reheated later. They're best filled with my Restaurant-Style Salsa (page 138) and plenty of cheese!

---

1 lb (455 g) venison steak, tenderloin or backstrap

1 tsp salt, divided

1 tsp pepper, divided

1 tbsp (15 ml) olive oil

4 eggs

1 tbsp (15 ml) milk (or nondairy milk of choice)

1 tbsp (15 g) butter

8 tortillas

½ cup (120 g) salsa, homemade (page 138) or store-bought

½ cup (86 g) cooked black beans

1 cup (113 g) grated pepper Jack cheese

Slice the venison against the grain into strips and sprinkle with ½ teaspoon of the salt and ½ teaspoon of the pepper. Heat the oil in a skillet over medium-high heat and then add the venison strips. Cook for about 5 minutes, until they're just browned all over. Remove the venison from the pan and set aside.

In a bowl, whisk together the eggs, milk, remaining ½ teaspoon of salt and remaining ½ teaspoon of pepper. Discard the olive oil in the pan, turn the heat to low, add the butter and let it melt. Add the eggs to the pan and scramble them. Right when they're set, remove the eggs from the pan and set them on a plate.

Lay out the tortillas and form an assembly line, adding the venison, eggs, salsa, black beans and cheese to each. Fold the bottom of the tortilla over the fillings, fold in the sides and roll up the burritos. Serve immediately or freeze.

If you're freezing the burritos, wrap each tightly in plastic wrap and store them in a zip-top bag. When you're ready to eat the frozen burritos, wrap them in a damp paper towel and microwave on high for 2 to 3 minutes.

Kale, Mushroom & Steak Frittata

Frittatas are an excellent dish for serving a crowd or for prepping breakfast for busy mornings. I love the hearty flavors of the mushrooms and venison steak, balanced out by the tangy goat cheese. Of course, if you want a dairy-free version, just omit the goat cheese.

This is another very flexible recipe. If you have chard or spinach and no kale, use what you have. This is also a great recipe for using up tougher cuts of steak, perhaps from leg meat, because you cube the venison and can remove any sinew.

1 tbsp (15 ml) olive oil

½ lb (226 g) venison steak

1½ tsp (9 g) salt, divided

1 tsp pepper, divided

8 eggs

¾ cup (180 ml) milk (or nondairy milk of choice)

2 cups (140 g) sliced baby bella mushrooms

3 to 4 cups (201 to 268 g) kale

4 oz (112 g) goat cheese, crumbled, divided

Preheat the oven to 350°F (180°C) and grease a 9 x 13–inch (23 x 33–cm) casserole dish.

Heat a large skillet over medium-high heat and add the oil. While the skillet heats, cube the steak into bite-size pieces, removing any sinew. Once the pan is hot, add the venison. Sprinkle ½ teaspoon of the salt and ½ teaspoon of the pepper all over the steak. Cook for 5 to 8 minutes, until the steak is browned all over. Remove it from the heat and set aside.

In a large bowl, whisk together the eggs, milk, remaining 1 teaspoon of salt and remaining ½ teaspoon of pepper. Fold in the mushrooms, kale, venison and 2 ounces (56 g) of the goat cheese. Pour the mixture into the prepared casserole dish. Sprinkle the remaining 2 ounces (56 g) of goat cheese all over the top of the frittata and bake for 45 to 50 minutes, or until the eggs are set.

Let it cool for about 10 minutes before slicing and serving.

Southern-Style Sausage Gravy

OK, you caught me. This isn't the lightest item on the menu in this book, but in my opinion, everyone needs a little stick-to-your-ribs breakfast once in a blue moon.

I used a really delicious spice blend here and some apple cider vinegar to brighten up the meat. You're absolutely going to love it. Serve with my Black Pepper Herb Biscuits (page 137).

2 tbsp (30 g) butter

1 lb (455 g) ground venison

1 tsp apple cider vinegar

1 tsp dried thyme

1 tsp salt

1 tsp pepper

⅓ cup (42 g) flour

3 cups (720 ml) whole milk

Homemade (page 137) or store-bought biscuits, to serve (optional)

Melt the butter in a large skillet (preferably cast iron) over medium heat. Add the venison and cook, stirring occasionally, until the venison is browned, 5 to 7 minutes. Add the vinegar, thyme, salt, pepper and flour. Cook, stirring frequently, for 3 minutes to cook out the raw flour taste.

Add the milk, stirring the mixture constantly so nothing sticks to the edges of the pan. This is why I like to use a cast-iron skillet—not as much sticking! Cook the gravy until the mixture has thickened, 5 to 7 minutes, and pour over warm biscuits.

Southwestern Venison Chorizo Quiche

SERVES 8

One thing to know about me is that I'm a sucker for pie. So, if I can have pie crust for breakfast, I'm all in.

I love serving quiche for a crowd, and I've made this for myself and reheated it all week, too. It's that perfect mix of delicate and hearty at the same time.

1 recipe Savory Pastry Dough (page 142)

6 eggs

½ cup (120 ml) milk (or nondairy milk of choice)

1 cup (240 g) cooked Venison Chorizo (page 39)

½ cup (75 g) chopped green bell pepper

½ cup (58 g) grated pepper Jack cheese

2 tbsp (30 g) salsa, homemade (page 138) or store-bought

¾ tsp salt

½ tsp black pepper

½ tsp garlic powder

Preheat the oven to 375°F (190°C).

Roll out the pastry dough and place it in a pie plate.

In a large bowl, whisk together the eggs and milk. Fold in the chorizo, bell pepper, cheese, salsa, salt, pepper and garlic powder. Pour the mixture into the unbaked pie shell and bake for 40 minutes, or until the eggs are set in the middle and the crust is golden. Serve warm with a hot cup of coffee.

Apple & Leek Hash with Sweet Potatoes

SERVES 6

GLUTEN FREE | DAIRY FREE |
30 MINUTES OR LESS

To me, a hash is an easy way to whip up a super balanced breakfast in a flash. I love using sweet potatoes for a healthy carbohydrate option. I also like veggies and a little bit of sweet in my hash. That's where the apples come in. The apples and paprika pair wonderfully with the ground venison. The only thing that makes this recipe better is a gooey fried egg on top.

1 tbsp (15 ml) olive oil

1 lb (455 g) ground venison

2 or 3 sweet potatoes, peeled and cubed (about 2 cups [240 g])

⅓ cup (80 ml) water

1 leek, washed and sliced

2 apples, diced

1 tbsp (15 ml) apple cider vinegar

1 tsp salt

½ tsp pepper

½ tsp onion powder

½ tsp garlic powder

¼ tsp smoked paprika or regular paprika

6 fried eggs, for serving (optional)

Heat the oil in a large skillet over medium-high heat. Add the venison and cook, stirring occasionally, until the venison is browned, 5 to 7 minutes. Remove the venison from the pan and set aside.

Add the sweet potatoes to the pan and sauté for about 5 minutes. Add the water and cover the skillet with a lid. Allow the potatoes to steam and soften for another 5 minutes.

Add the leek to the pan and sauté for 2 minutes, then add the apples, vinegar, salt, pepper, onion powder, garlic powder and paprika and stir to combine. Add the venison back to the skillet, stir and cook for 5 to 7 minutes longer, until the sweet potatoes, leeks and apples are soft. Remove from the heat and serve as is, or with a fried egg per serving.

NOTE: This hash stores very well in the fridge for about a week or in the freezer for about 2 months.

Steak & Eggs

SERVES 1

GLUTEN FREE | DAIRY FREE | 30 MINUTES OR LESS

Steak and eggs—is there a better stick-to-your-ribs breakfast option out there? It's one of those meals to make when you have a long day ahead of you, especially if you have a long day in the tree stand.

I prefer my steak and eggs with fried or sunny-side-up eggs with plenty of runny yolk action. Venison steak is leaner than beef, so for me, it's a better option. I like this best with a squeeze of lemon to brighten things up. My Herb Roasted Potatoes (page 145) are the perfect thing to serve alongside this dish!

¼ to ½ lb (112 to 226 g) venison steak

¾ tsp salt, divided

½ tsp pepper, divided

2 tbsp (30 g) butter, divided

2 eggs

1 lemon wedge

Season the steak with ½ teaspoon of the salt and ¼ teaspoon of the pepper.

Melt 1 tablespoon (15 g) of the butter in a large skillet (preferably cast iron) over medium-high heat. Place the steak in the skillet and cook for 3 to 5 minutes per side, or until the internal temperature reaches 125 to 130°F (52 to 54°C) on a meat thermometer. Remove the steak from the skillet and let it rest while you make the eggs.

Wipe the skillet out or use a different one if you need to. Turn the heat to low and add the remaining 1 tablespoon (15 g) of butter to the skillet. Crack the eggs into the skillet and let them cook to your desired level of doneness. Sprinkle them with the remaining ¼ teaspoon of salt and remaining ¼ teaspoon of pepper. Serve immediately with the lemon wedge on the side.

Sauces &
Marinades

This chapter is full of my favorite marinades and sauces to pair with venison. A few simple flavor profiles can really transform deer meat into something wonderful.

A lot of the recipes in this book use the All-Purpose Marinade and Homemade Venison Stock. These two will be staples in your kitchen.

All-Purpose Marinade

MAKES ABOUT ½ CUP (120 ML),
ENOUGH TO MARINATE 1 TO 2 LBS
(455 TO 910 G) OF MEAT
GLUTEN FREE | DAIRY FREE

Ah, the all-purpose marinade. I've been messing around with venison marinades for some time now. I think it's important to have something you can whisk together in a pinch. I've tried crazier ingredients like hot sauces, maple syrup, mustard and more, but I keep coming back to this bright, fresh and simple version.

This is a great marinade to use on tenderloin, backstrap, chops, steaks—really any cut—and especially those that are tougher in nature. The acid helps break down the tissue and tenderize the meat. Everyone who has ever tried this recipe has given glowing reviews.

¼ cup (60 ml) olive oil

2 tbsp (30 ml) red wine vinegar

Juice of ½ lemon

3 cloves garlic, smashed and minced

1 tsp Italian seasoning

¾ tsp salt

½ tsp pepper

Add all of the ingredients to a jar with a lid or a bowl and shake or whisk together vigorously.

Add the meat you want to marinate to a bowl or zip-top bag and pour the marinade over. Let it sit in the fridge for at least 1 hour, or up to overnight, before cooking.

Homemade Venison Stock

MAKES ABOUT 1 GALLON (3.6 L)

GLUTEN FREE | DAIRY FREE

When I can, I like to make my own cooking stocks at home. Good stock is expensive, but it's a nonnegotiable ingredient in my kitchen. Making it myself saves me a lot of money. Many of my recipes use stock, so it's important to have the good stuff on hand. When I make my own stock, I let it cook, skim off the fat and then divide it into 4-cup (960-ml) portions. The stock gets stored in the freezer, and I'm able to snag some when I need it. It's really a set-it-and-forget-it type of thing that's worth doing on your own. Save your cooking scraps and store them in a freezer-safe zip-top bag until you're ready to make stock.

About 2 lbs (910 g) deer bones (I like knucklebones—they're nice and rich in gelatin)

2 onions, halved

1 garlic bulb, halved

3 celery ribs, roughly chopped

2 carrots, roughly chopped

2 tsp (12 g) salt

1 tsp peppercorns

1 tbsp (15 ml) apple cider vinegar

2 or 3 sprigs fresh herbs, such as thyme or bay leaves (optional)

Add all of the ingredients to a large stockpot. Nothing needs to be nicely chopped and you can add the onion and garlic peels. More flavor! Fill the pot up with water so that everything is almost submerged. Place the stockpot on the stove, turn the heat to high and cover the pot. Once the broth is boiling, turn the heat down to low and allow the broth to simmer for 4 to 12 hours. The longer it simmers, the richer the broth will be.

When you're done cooking, remove the pot from the heat and let it cool. I like to refrigerate the pot overnight so the fat coagulates on the top and I can scrape it off.

Once you remove the fat, strain the broth and discard everything but the liquid. Divide the stock into 2- or 4-cup (480- or 960-ml) portions and store for a week in the fridge or for 6 months in the freezer.

NOTE: You can roast the bones before you make this stock, but it's not necessary. It just provides more flavor. You can also use frozen bones for this recipe; there's no need to defrost before making this, as they will defrost during the cooking process.

Curry Marinade

MAKES ABOUT ½ CUP (120 ML),
ENOUGH FOR ABOUT 2 LBS (910 G) OF MEAT
GLUTEN FREE | DAIRY FREE

This curry marinade manages to be cozy and bright at the same time. It's wonderful to use on steaks or chops, or even a whole tenderloin if you want something different. The blend of spices and the splash of vinegar give venison a whole lot of interest.

¼ cup (60 ml) olive oil

3 tbsp (45 ml) white wine vinegar

Juice of 1 lime

3 cloves garlic, smashed and minced

½" (1.3-cm) piece fresh ginger, peeled and grated

2 tsp (4 g) curry powder

1 tsp salt

½ tsp pepper

½ tsp ground coriander

Add all of the ingredients to a jar with a lid or a bowl and shake or whisk together vigorously.

Add the meat you want to marinate to a bowl or zip-top bag and pour the marinade over. Let it sit in the fridge for at least 1 hour, or up to overnight, before cooking.

Chimichurri Marinade

Cilantro can be quite a polarizing ingredient—you either love it or hate it. I happen to love it! It's such a bright and refreshing herb that stands up wonderfully to the flavor of venison.

I love whipping up a quick batch of this recipe and marinating steaks for the grill. It can also be served on the side as a sauce. Check out my Chimichurri-Marinated Steak with Fresh Salsa recipe on page 51 for a deliciously quick dinner idea.

1 cup (16 g) fresh cilantro

5 cloves garlic

¼ cup (60 ml) olive oil

2 tbsp (30 ml) red wine vinegar

½ tsp salt

½ tsp pepper

Add all of the ingredients to a small food processor or blender. Process until the mixture is smooth and the cilantro has broken down.

Marinate steaks and chops for at least 1 hour and up to overnight in this delicious chimichurri. Or serve alongside a dish as a sauce.

Blueberry Balsamic Reduction

MAKES ABOUT 1 CUP (240 ML)

GLUTEN FREE | DAIRY FREE

Dark berries and balsamic play very well in the sandbox with venison. This reduction is an easy upgrade for steaks or my Roasted Whole Tenderloin with Peppercorns (page 31). It's one of those sauces you can forget about on the stove while you prep the remainder of a meal, but you'll be well rewarded for whipping up a batch.

2 tsp (10 ml) olive oil

1 clove garlic, minced

3 cups (440 g) blueberries

¼ cup (60 ml) balsamic vinegar

3 tbsp (45 g) sugar

1 tsp salt

Pinch of nutmeg (freshly grated is best)

Warm the olive oil in a medium saucepan over medium heat. Add the garlic and sauté for 2 minutes. Add the blueberries and cook, stirring occasionally, until the blueberries burst and the mixture starts to boil. Add the vinegar, sugar and salt. Bring the mixture to a boil again, and then turn the heat down to low and let the sauce simmer until the mixture has reduced by about half, about 20 minutes. Taste to check the seasoning level. Add the nutmeg and transfer the sauce to a small bowl or gravy boat for serving.

Five-Spice Marinade

MAKES ½ CUP (120 ML), ENOUGH TO
MARINATE ABOUT 2 LBS (910 G) OF MEAT
GLUTEN FREE | DAIRY FREE

This is a flavor-packed little marinade I like to use when I need to shake up our routine at home for weeknight meals. Chinese five-spice can be found in many grocery stores or ordered online, and I love it because it's packed with peppercorns, anise, cloves, cinnamon and fennel. The result is a really warm spice blend that pairs beautifully with venison.

You can use this marinade with steaks, chops or even large cuts of meat if you're trying to bring the funk. Try it out in my Asian Chop Salad (page 91) as well.

¼ cup (60 ml) olive oil

¼ cup (60 ml) soy sauce (or coconut aminos for soy/gluten free)

2 tbsp (30 ml) rice wine vinegar or white wine vinegar

1 tbsp (15 ml) hoisin sauce

1 tsp Chinese five-spice powder

½ tsp garlic powder

Add all of the ingredients to a jar with a lid or a bowl and shake or whisk together vigorously.

Add the meat you want to marinate to a bowl or zip-top bag and pour the marinade over. Let it sit in the fridge for at least 1 hour, or up to overnight, before cooking.

Sides

While these recipes don't contain venison, this book would be incomplete without them. These are the sides that pair perfectly with all of the dishes in this book. I wanted you to have one place to reference to make a killer wild-game meal.

Black Pepper Herb Biscuits

MAKES 8 BISCUITS

To tell you the truth, these biscuits are pillowy clouds of buttery heaven. Do you need more convincing to try them?

I love adding little twists to classic biscuits. Not enough to totally alter the original flavor, just enough to enhance them. Black pepper, sage and thyme also marry beautifully with venison. I love these because they pair perfectly with breakfast items, such as my Southern-Style Sausage Gravy (page 112), and supper things, like my Roasted Whole Tenderloin with Peppercorns (page 31).

½ cup (112 g [1 stick]) cold butter

2 cups (250 g) all-purpose flour

1 tbsp (14 g) baking powder

2 tbsp (30 g) sugar, plus more for sprinkling

1 tsp salt, plus more for sprinkling

½ tsp black pepper, plus more for sprinkling

¼ tsp dried thyme

¼ tsp dried sage

¾ cup (180 ml) plus 1 tbsp (15 ml) half-and-half, divided

1 tsp apple cider vinegar

Preheat the oven to 425°F (220°C). Line a baking sheet with parchment paper or a Silpat. Place the butter in the freezer for about 15 minutes to get it really cold.

In a large bowl, whisk together the flour, baking powder, sugar, salt, pepper, thyme and sage.

Once the butter is good and cold, grate the entire stick right into the flour mixture. If you're left with a little nub, just tear it apart with your fingers. Work the butter into the flour quickly, making the mixture into a coarse meal. You want to work quickly so the warmth of your hands doesn't melt the butter. It's OK if you have a few lumps.

In a small bowl, combine ¾ cup (180 ml) of the half-and-half and cider vinegar and add it gradually to the flour and butter mixture. Use a spatula to fold it in until it just combines into a blob (very scientific, no?). You don't want it gloopy and wet, or so dry that it won't stick together.

Turn the dough out onto a floured surface. You won't need a rolling pin if you work quickly, just your hands. Flatten the dough with your fingertips into a rectangle and fold it in half. Press it out again into a rectangle and fold it in half again. Repeat this three more times. This creates those layers.

Shape the dough into a rectangle with your fingers again. Using a floured round cookie or biscuit cutter, cut out rounds of dough and place them on the prepared baking sheet.

Brush the biscuits with the remaining 1 tablespoon (15 ml) of half-and-half, and then sprinkle the biscuits sparingly with sugar, salt and black pepper—just enough to lightly dust them. Bake for 12 to 14 minutes, or until golden brown.

Restaurant-Style Salsa

MAKES ABOUT 2 CUPS (480 ML)

GLUTEN FREE | DAIRY FREE |
30 MINUTES OR LESS

There's NOTHING like tucking yourself into a little booth at a Mexican joint and getting that first bowl of warm tortilla chips and salsa. The salsa at restaurants is just . . . better. It's traditionally thinner, and really fresh. I can't get enough, and I usually end up filling up on chips and salsa before my meal comes. Sound familiar?

I know it's easy to go to the store to grab a jar of salsa, but making your own can really take some of the dishes in this cookbook to the next level, like the Barbacoa Meat (page 47) and the Huevos Rancheros (page 100).

3 jalapeño peppers

½ onion, chopped

3 cloves garlic

2 (10-oz [280-g]) cans diced tomatoes
with green chiles, drained

¾ tsp salt

Juice of 1 lime

Hold the jalapeños carefully with tongs over an open flame on the stove or place them on a baking sheet under the broiler for a few minutes. Use caution while doing this. When the skin on the jalapeños starts to bubble and blacken on all sides, they're done. This should only take about 5 minutes. Let the jalapeños cool a bit.

Add the onion, garlic, tomatoes, salt and lime juice to a small food processor or high-powered blender.

Once the jalapeños have cooled enough for you to handle them, slice off the tops and cut them in half. Carefully remove the seeds. You may want to use gloves to do this because jalapeños can burn your skin, eyes and mouth. Add the jalapeños to the food processor or blender, being sure to add any charred bits that come off in the seeding process (that's the flavor). Pulse the salsa mixture until your desired texture is reached, stirring in between pulses. Pour the salsa into a jar. This will keep in the fridge for 5 to 7 days.

Favorite Simple Salad

SERVES 4
GLUTEN FREE | 30 MINUTES OR LESS

I can't count the number of times I have made this salad. It's referred to in our house as "the salad." I almost always whip it up when we have a heavy meal like my Perfect Roast with Garlic and Herbs (page 19) or Red Wine–Braised Short Ribs with Herb Gremolata (page 35). It balances out the richness and gives you some added veggies.

People who tend to cover salads in a lot of dressing are often surprised when they see this one at the table, but I really encourage you to try it. Even my ranch-loving husband goes crazy for it. Large ribbons of fresh Parmesan are a must! You can add chopped carrots, tomatoes, cucumber—whatever you like—but just lettuce is also delicious.

4 cups (120 g) chopped romaine lettuce or other leafy greens

2 to 3 tsp (10 to 15 ml) best-quality olive oil

2 tsp (10 ml) lemon juice or to taste

½ to ¾ tsp salt or to taste

½ tsp freshly ground black pepper

¼ cup (25 g) Parmesan ribbons (I shave mine with a vegetable peeler)

Add the romaine to a large bowl and drizzle it with the olive oil and lemon juice, then sprinkle with the salt and pepper. Use a light hand when adding everything. You can always taste and add more of something. Toss everything together and give it a taste. Now is the time to add more acid or salt if you'd like. Add the shaved Parmesan on top and serve.

Savory Pastry Dough

MAKES 1 CRUST

I love making pastry dough. Pie is one of my favorite things to bake, so I always have some sweet and savory pastry dough on hand for pies, quiches and tarts.

I love this recipe because of the black pepper and olive oil. It has such an incredible flavor that works perfectly with my Southwestern Venison Chorizo Quiche (page 115), or you can turn the Kale, Mushroom & Steak Frittata (page 111) into a quiche. This would also be wonderful for a venison steak pie!

1½ cups (188 g) all-purpose flour

½ tsp salt

¼ tsp pepper

6 tbsp (90 g) very cold butter, cubed

2 tbsp (30 ml) olive oil

2 to 3 tbsp (30 to 45 ml) ice water, or as needed

If you have a food processor, that's the best way to assemble this dough. If not, simply use a pastry cutter or fork to cut the butter into the flour.

In a food processor, add the flour, salt and pepper and pulse them together. Add the butter and pulse a few times until it is broken down into pea-size pieces. Add the olive oil and water, a little at a time, and pulse until the dough comes together into a ball. Remove it from the food processor, wrap it lightly in plastic wrap and let it rest in the fridge for 30 minutes before rolling it out and using it in a recipe.

Herb Roasted Potatoes

I'm not sure that there's a better combination than meat and potatoes, and venison sure fits right into the equation. This is my favorite, simple way to make roasted potatoes that pair perfectly with almost every single meal.

3 to 4 cups (360 to 480 g) diced gold potatoes

1 tbsp (15 ml) olive oil

1 tbsp (15 ml) melted butter

3 cloves garlic, minced

1 tsp salt

½ tsp pepper

2 tsp (2 g) chopped fresh rosemary

2 tsp (2 g) chopped fresh thyme

2 tsp (3 g) chopped fresh parsley

Preheat the oven to 400°F (200°C) and get out a large baking sheet.

Spread the potatoes on the baking sheet in an even layer. Drizzle over the olive oil and butter and toss the potatoes well to cover them. The combination of olive oil and butter makes the potatoes both crispy and tasty. Sprinkle on the garlic, salt, pepper, rosemary and thyme and toss the potatoes again so they're evenly coated.

Roast the potatoes for 30 to 35 minutes, turning them a few times during the cooking process to help them roast evenly, until golden brown and slightly crispy on the edges. Sprinkle with the parsley and serve them hot and fresh out of the oven.

Best Ever Stovetop Broccoli

SERVES 4

GLUTEN FREE | DAIRY FREE |
30 MINUTES OR LESS

I started making broccoli this way a few years ago and it comes out perfectly every time. When you just sauté broccoli, sometimes it gets too charred but is still undercooked inside, and steaming broccoli makes it too soggy, in my opinion. I sauté it for about 2 minutes, add a little bit of water to the pan and DON'T cover it. It sautés and steams and it's such a cinch to make.

We have broccoli as a side at least once a week, and it goes with almost anything in this book.

If you're not a big fan of lemon, just omit the lemon zest, and give a floret a taste before serving to test the seasoning level.

1 head broccoli

1 tbsp (15 ml) olive oil

About 2 tbsp (30 ml) water

¼ tsp lemon zest

½ tsp lemon juice

¼ to ½ tsp salt

¼ to ½ tsp pepper

Chop the florets off of the broccoli and into bite-size pieces. You can chop the stems into bite-size pieces if you wish to use them. I happen to love them.

Heat the olive oil in a large skillet or wok over medium heat. Add the broccoli and sauté for about 2 minutes, and then add the water. Stir, moving the broccoli frequently, and don't cover it. The water will steam and soften the broccoli a bit, making it perfectly tender.

Add the lemon zest, juice, salt and pepper, and cook, still stirring frequently, until all of the liquid evaporates, 4 to 5 minutes. Remove the broccoli from the heat and serve.

Couscous Salad with Tomatoes & Cucumbers

SERVES 4 TO 6

DAIRY FREE | 30 MINUTES OR LESS

Whenever I want a bright and fresh side, this is always my go-to. It's wonderful to whip up in the summer with garden-fresh tomatoes, but I can almost always find the ingredients in the middle of winter if I need a break from heavy stews and roasts.

This is the perfect dish to pair with my Kebabs with Tahini-Yogurt Sauce (page 43), Chimichurri-Marinated Steak with Fresh Salsa (page 51) or even my Herby Mediterranean Pita Salad (page 92).

2 cups (480 ml) water

1 (5.8-oz [162-g]) box couscous

3 tbsp (45 ml) olive oil, divided

1½ tsp (9 g) salt, divided

2 cups (300 g) cherry tomatoes

1 large English cucumber

1 tsp lemon juice

1 tbsp (15 ml) red wine vinegar

½ tsp pepper

Bring the water to a boil in a medium-size saucepan and add the couscous, 1 tablespoon (15 ml) of the olive oil and ½ teaspoon of the salt. Stir everything together well and remove the couscous from the heat. Cover the pot with a lid and let it sit for 5 minutes, then fluff the couscous with a fork.

While the couscous is sitting, halve the tomatoes and dice the cucumber. Add the veggies to a bowl and add the remaining 2 tablespoons (30 ml) of olive oil, remaining 1 teaspoon of salt, lemon juice, vinegar and pepper. Add the fluffed couscous and stir to combine. Serve hot, at room temperature or cold.

Pickled Red Onion

MAKES 2 CUPS (320 G)

GLUTEN FREE | DAIRY FREE

I absolutely love pickled and briny flavors, so pickled red onion is a favorite of mine. I think it's the perfect thing to serve with venison to enhance and cut through the rich flavor.

I recommend making a jar and saving it in the fridge to serve with Huevos Rancheros (page 100) or Barbacoa Meat (page 47). You'll be glad you did.

1 large red onion

¾ cup (180 ml) water

¾ cup (180 ml) distilled white vinegar

2 tsp (12 g) salt

1 tbsp (15 g) sugar

2 cloves garlic, smashed

½ tsp peppercorns

Pinch of smoked paprika (optional)

Slice the onion thinly and layer the slices in a 16-ounce (480-ml) glass jar with a lid. Set the jar aside.

In a medium saucepan over medium-high heat, combine the water, vinegar, salt, sugar, garlic, peppercorns and smoked paprika, if using. Cook until the mixture just starts to boil and the salt and sugar dissolve. Remove the saucepan from the heat and pour the pickling liquid over the onions in the jar.

Place the onions in the fridge to cool for about 2 hours and serve as desired. These will keep well for about 2 weeks.

Acknowledgments

I'll never forget my first phone call with Page Street Publishing. After sending my book proposal for review, we kicked around the ideas I had for this book, and they finally said, "We think you have a market for this book, and we're going to be sending over an offer." After I picked my jaw up off the floor, I was filled with immense gratitude for this special company that would take a chance on me, a first-time author, so that I could provide my readers with a product I believe in. So, thank you to Page Street Publishing for allowing me to reach others and show them how to work with venison every day.

But, first and foremost, a huge thanks to my husband, Jared: You provided almost all of the meat I use to create my recipes. Thank you for the extra help testing, brainstorming, dishwashing and house cleaning during the cookbook creation process. Since I started Miss Allie's Kitchen almost four years ago, you have been my constant and steady supporter. Whatever I need to do to invest in my business, you're right behind me, encouraging me to grow. You're always willing to share your vast knowledge of the outdoors, hunting and deer processing, and I am beyond thankful we've had the chance to share this experience. This book is as much yours as it is mine.

To my parents: Thank you for encouraging my ferocious love for food and all things creative. Through your words and example, I have had the pillars to stabilize success. You both always encouraged me from a young age to take my own path, and I owe all of this opportunity to you.

To my in-laws: Thank you both for all of your excitement and assistance. You were so kind to share your supply of deer meat when ours was low, a kindness I will never forget. Joe, thank you for sharing your love of the outdoors and expertise with Jared. It is something we will treasure and pass on.

To Nicole and Dan Culver, my amazing business coaches: Without you, I never would have thought to approach Page Street with an idea for a book. It's because of you that I'm sitting here writing this. I'm genuinely not sure where I would be without your guidance and knowledge. You impact so many lives, and you have helped my dreams come true.

To our friends Chris and Kayla and our family friend Brian: You so kindly gifted us with a supply of venison when ours was getting low during the recipe-testing process. Thank you for that beautiful display of selflessness!

And finally, to my readers at Miss Allie's Kitchen: You all are truly the reason I was able to write this book. Your excitement and engagement gets me up and running on the days when I'm not sure how to keep on. Your genuine interest in the Miss Allie's Kitchen brand has taken me to places I never could have imagined. Each and every one of you has a place in my story, and for that I'll always be thankful.

A heartfelt thanks to all who have supported me on this journey!

About the Author

Allie Doran is the creator of Miss Allie's Kitchen, a food and lifestyle brand that brings whole food, wild game, baking and cocktail content directly to her amazing readers. By craft, she's a food writer and photographer, so you can almost always find her in the kitchen testing and photographing new recipes. Allie's recipes have been featured in *North American Whitetail* magazine, BuzzFeed, HuffPost and the feedfeed. Allie has dreamed about writing her own cookbook since she was a teenager and purchased her first cookbook—all about pie.

When Allie is not in the kitchen, you can find her exploring the great outdoors with her husband, Jared, or on horseback. Allie and her family live in a small central Pennsylvania town, but she enjoys traveling to the city from time to time to try out new restaurants, and she's a self-proclaimed wine aficionado.

For more about Allie, connect with her on her website, www.missallieskitchen.com, or on her Instagram page, @miss.allieskitchen.

Index